THE MYTHIC TAROT

Also by Juliet Sharman-Burke
The Complete Book of Tarot
The Mythic Tarot Workbook
The Mythic Journey (with Liz Greene)
Understanding the Tarot
Mastering the Tarot
Beginner's Guide to Tarot

Also by Liz Greene
Saturn: A New Look at an Old Devil
Relating: An Astrological Guide to Living with Others
Astrology for Lovers
The Outer Planets and their Cycles: The Astrology of the Collective
The Jupiter-Saturn Conference Lectures (with Stephen Arroyo)
Looking at Astrology (for children)
The Astrology of Fate
The Development of the Personality (with Howard Sasportas)
The Dreamer of the Vine (fiction)
The Puppet-Master (fiction)

THE MYTHIC TAROT

JULIET SHARMAN-BURKE
AND LIZ GREENE

CARDS ILLUSTRATED BY
TRICIA NEWELL

To Emily Kate, with love
Für Alois, der die besten Eigenschaften der Könige
der Kelche und Münzen in sich vereint, in Liebe.

Text copyright © Juliet Sharman-Burke and Liz Greene 1986
Illustrations copyright © Tricia Newell 1986
This edition copyright © Eddison Sadd Editions Limited 1986

All rights reserved. No part of this work may be reproduced or utilized in any form or by any means, electronic or mechanical including photocopying, recording, or by any information storage and retrieval system, without the prior written agreement of the publisher.

First published in Canada in 1986 by Methuen Publications

Distributed in Canada by:
Fitzhenry & Whiteside Ltd.
195 Allstate Parkway,
Markham, ON
L3R 4T8

National Library of Canada Cataloguing in Publication Data

Sharman-Burke, Juliet
   The mythic tarot [kit]
Includes a book, a ritual cloth and a deck of tarot cards.
Includes bibliographical references.
ISBN 0-7737-3328-0 Rev. Ed. ISBN 1-55005-097-4
   1. Tarot. I. Greene, Liz II. Newell, Tricia III. Title.
BF1879.T2S53 2001   133.3'2424   C2001-900928-3

AN EDDISON•SADD EDITION
Edited, designed and produced by
Eddison Sadd Editions Limited
St Chad's House, 148 King's Cross Road,
London WC1X 9DH

Phototypeset by Bookworm Typesetting, Manchester, England
Origination by Columbia Offset, Singapore
Produced in China

CONTENTS

INTRODUCTION	6	**THE MINOR ARCANA**	84

The Origins of the Tarot Cards	6
The Mythic Tarot	10

THE MAJOR ARCANA	**14**

The Fool	18
The Magician	21
The Empress	24
The Emperor	27
The High Priestess	30
The Hierophant	33
The Lovers	36
The Chariot	39
Justice	42
Temperance	45
Strength	48
The Hermit	51
The Wheel of Fortune	54
The Hanged Man	57
Death	60
The Devil	63
The Tower	66
The Star	69
The Moon	72
The Sun	75
Judgement	78
The World	81

The Four Suits	84
THE SUIT OF CUPS	
The Numbered Cards	91
The Court Cards	105
THE SUIT OF WANDS	
The Numbered Cards	117
The Court Cards	132
THE SUIT OF SWORDS	
The Numbered Cards	143
The Court Cards	159
THE SUIT OF PENTACLES	
The Numbered Cards	171
The Court Cards	187

READING THE CARDS	**196**

What the Tarot Can and Cannot Do	196
Making a Relationship With the Cards	198
Laying Out a Spread	199
Reading the Spread	200
Two Example Spreads	204
Conclusion	214

FURTHER READING	216
ACKNOWLEDGEMENTS	216

INTRODUCTION

The Origins of the Tarot Cards

The origins of the Tarot cards – who first designed them, where, when, and for what purpose – remain vague and elusive despite a considerable number of books and articles which over the years have attempted to illuminate the darkness in which the cards are shrouded. The perennial enchantment of the cards is evidenced not only by these sometimes sound and scholarly and sometimes wildly mystical writings, but also by the fascination which the Tarot cards continue to hold for the layman despite endless attempts on the part of the sceptic to make fun of them and relegate them to the general dustbin of tea-leaf readings, crystal balls and other oddities. Whatever it is about the Tarot cards, they have held the human imagination for at least five hundred years and possibly for much longer; and they certainly show no sign of disappearing.

What is it about these strange picture-cards which continues to exercise such a mysterious spell, even over those individuals who consider themselves sensible and not ordinarily prone to believing in occult mysteries? In part, the answer to this may be that the Tarot cards are not 'occult' – that is, they are not supernatural or magical in the sense that those words are generally used, and they are not the especial property of the esoteric initiate, although many Tarot students would like to think so. There is evidence to suggest that in the mid-fifteenth century – the time scholars believe the cards were first in evidence in Europe – they were freely available to anyone who could afford a deck and who cared to make the effort to understand and use them. It is our intention in this book to restore the Tarot cards to their original accessibility, so that they need no longer remain the domain of the scholar or occultist who deliberately obfuscates their symbolism.

Writers on the subject of the Tarot have at one time or another assigned the invention of the cards to a wide range of sources. Some claim their origins lie in the religious rituals and symbols of the ancient Egyptians; others suggest that they spring from the mystery cults of Mithras in the first centuries after Christ. Still others find concurrences

INTRODUCTION

with pagan Celtic beliefs, or with the romantic poetry cycles of the Holy Grail which emerged during the Middle Ages in Western Europe. More sober scholars, relying upon what may be seen and touched in museums, focus on the earliest cards we now possess, and believe they were painted during the Renaissance. Certainly if we wish to base our exploration of the Tarot's origins exclusively on factual evidence, the first documented decks of Tarot cards – those which include not only the ordinary four suits of playing cards, but also the strange images of what are now known as the Major Arcana or Tarot Trumps – spring from the second half of the fifteenth century and were painted in Italy. There are two of these decks, one known as the Charles VI pack and the other known as the Visconti-Sforza pack. But the existence of these two beautifully designed decks of Tarot cards does not really tell us anything with any certainty. They are simply all that we can hold in our hands. And if these are indeed the first invention of the Tarot, this historical documentation cannot reveal why we in the modern era, who have long ago left behind the peculiar beliefs and world-view of the Renaissance, should still find that the symbols and images of the cards hold such an inexplicable air of profound significance. These picture-cards seem to invoke elusive memories and half-known associations with myth, legend and folklore, and imply despite rational objection some kind of story or secret which cannot be totally formulated and which slips away the moment we attempt to define it too rigidly.

The Italian Renaissance encompassed a revival of classical Greek thought with its dynamic spirit of experiment, adventure and enterprise. From the grey, rigid, melancholy world-view of the Middle Ages, the bright animistic soul of ancient Greece burst upon the Western world with enormous energy and incalculable consequences. Greek manuscripts – particularly the writings of Plato and the Neoplatonists and Hermetic philosophers of Alexandria and the Middle East – found their way into the West after the sacking of Constantinople by the Turks in 1453. These manuscripts, which had been unavailable in Western Europe since the Goths overran Rome, arrived in Florence at a time when that city's rulers were sympathetic to such heretical writings, and the new spirit was rapidly spread by the recently invented printing

INTRODUCTION

press. This Neoplatonic-Hermetic movement boldly challenged beliefs which had for many centuries been considered sacrosanct, for it flew directly in the face of the Church's authority, decrying blind obedience to dogma, and encouraging the psychological development of the individual. The vision was as pagan as it was Christian, and images of the ancient gods and goddesses began to appear in Renaissance art where before there had been only conventional religious themes. And it first flooded Western Europe at precisely the time that the earliest known Tarot cards were in use.

We need to know a little of what this new Neoplatonic-Hermetic world-view espoused, because we can then understand the meaning of the Tarot cards better. Also, we can begin to glimpse just why the cards fell into such disrepute, and were associated with the work of the Devil. Essentially, the new world-view challenged the old medieval idea that man was a poor, sinful creature who could only know God through His intermediary, the Church. 'What a great miracle is man!' became the rallying cry of the Renaissance, for in the new vision man was a proud co-creator in God's cosmos. The Neoplatonic-Hermetic movement believed that the human being was in essence a microcosm of the greater universe, and that therefore self-knowledge – knowledge of the soul – was the only true religious path through which one might reconnect with one's divine origins. Self-knowledge was of course the first dictum of the Greeks; 'Know thyself' was carved above the doorway of Apollo's temple at Delphi. And knowledge of self meant knowledge of the many diverse drives and impulses of the inner man or woman, some of them dark as well as light, as well as knowledge of the cycles of development at work in human life. The multiplicity of Greek gods seemed, to the newly awakened mind of the Renaissance, a better and more truthful analogy of the complex patterns of the universe than the rather static world of the Trinity with its exclusively male and beneficent deity. Moreover, if man was a great miracle and a co-creator in the cosmos, then he had the right to tamper with himself and his world, even improving upon God's not-so-perfect creation, rather than obediently accepting his lot according to religious dogma. It is no wonder that the Church retaliated with such great ferocity, eventually

INTRODUCTION

forcing this new vision underground in the ensuing two centuries.

Along with the sparkling and multifaceted Greek gods, the Renaissance also adopted a Greek method of approaching the gods: the art of memory-systems which were initially developed as a kind of pictorial key to meditation. Whether the individual simply wished to remember the text of a speech or poem, or wished to experience a feeling of the connectedness of the soul with the larger universe, these systems involved study or meditation upon a series of magical images, each of which was a symbol and therefore had several levels of meaning. An example of memory systems still in use today is the Stations of the Cross found in Catholic churches, intended to recreate in the mind and heart of the observer the whole unfolding story of Christ's life, death and resurrection. During the Renaissance, the memory-systems became associated with magical talismans or emblems, pictures or amulets meant to invoke in the observer a sense of a certain power at work in life on many levels. The object of such meditation was to form a kind of ladder to reach higher levels of consciousness and gain insights into the divine world. The images of the Greek gods which appear in paintings, such as those of Botticelli as well as in the early Tarot decks, are not mere revivals of pagan worship. They were considered to be symbols of great laws at work through the whole of creation. Meditation on these images was meant to restore 'memory' of the divine world of the soul, raising individual consciousness from its entrapment in the mundane trivia of the material world and reconnecting the person with his or her real source.

The Church naturally considered such traffic with pagan images to be the work of the Devil, and energetically suppressed every study which touched upon such heretical themes. By the time the so-called Age of Enlightenment had dawned, ushering the 'scientific' world-view that apparently put paid to the mystical nonsense of earlier centuries, the Tarot cards had been relegated to life in the shadow-world of the occultists of the eighteenth and nineteenth centuries. No longer accessible to the public and no longer relevant to any philosophical or spiritual world-view acceptable in society, the cards were progressively doctored and changed in accordance with the particular spiritual beliefs

INTRODUCTION

of the group or order which had got hold of them. Thus the Tarot cards as we now usually see them are interesting hybrids, influenced by everything from Cabalistic thought to Arthurian legends, from latter-day magical practises to Rosicrucian symbolism. Interesting though these hybrids are, they have lost their original universality, and the average reader, desiring to learn more about the cards, is often put off by the obscure symbolism and sometimes rigid moral and spiritual doctrine which has been injected by a particular esoteric school of thought.

The Mythic Tarot

We have attempted to restore some of the original simplicity and accessibility of the Tarot cards by redesigning the deck in accord with the images of the Greek gods so beloved by Renaissance artists and writers, and which form the cultural underpinning of Western life. The Greek gods are not the exclusive property of any particular esoteric school, religious doctrine, or spiritual path. Amoral yet containing profound moral truths, they predate and permeate our modern Judaeo-Christian religious symbols as well as the art and literature of the whole of Western culture; and they remain the most fundamental and precise images to describe the many-sided and multicoloured workings of the human psyche. They are symbols of raw nature, our own raw human nature with its deep ambivalence of body and spirit and its mutually contradictory drives toward self-realization and unconsciousness. Our understanding of our own ambivalence has only recently begun to be restored to its ancient scope by modern depth psychology, which inevitably has had to return to the source – the pagan gods – for its understanding of human behaviour. Thus, in both book and cards, we have adhered to the traditional meanings of the cards, while at the same time resurrecting the old gods who have been buried beneath centuries of embellishment.

What, then, is myth? Our dictionaries offer several definitions. One is that myth is an untrue story – a perspective which is no doubt valid in

INTRODUCTION

one sense, but sadly inept in another. Certainly no archaeologist has ever found the bones of Oedipus or Hercules. But what may be untrue in concrete terms may be true on an inner level, as a type of subjective experience. The word myth can also imply a scheme or plan, and it is this meaning which we must consider when we look at the Tarot cards. Mythic images are really spontaneous pictures, sprung from the human imagination, which describe in poetic language essential human experiences and essential human patterns of development. Psychology now uses the term 'archetypal' to describe these patterns. Archetypal means a pattern which is universal and existent in all people in all cultures at all periods of history.

Birth, for example, is an archetypal experience. This is obviously true on a concrete level – we have all, at one time or another, been born. But it is also a psychological experience of an archetypal kind, because every time we begin something new, or enter a new phase of life, there is a sense of birth. And birth also implies other subjective states, because being born means leaving the comforting and serene waters of the maternal womb, whether this is on a physical level or a psychological one. Death is also an archetypal experience; we will all, one day, die. But death likewise is psychological, because life changes and we ourselves change, and each time there is an ending of any kind, a separation or the end of a phase of life, there is a sense of death. Puberty, the passage from childhood into manhood or womanhood, is also archetypal. We all pass through the profound physical and emotional stages of puberty between around twelve and fifteen years of age. But we may also make this passage many times during life on an inner, subjective level, each time we move from an essentially childish and naive way of viewing things to a full embracing of life which penetrates and deepens us. For this reason, a myth such as the abduction of the maiden Persephone from her mother by the underworld god Hades is both an image of the process of puberty with its terrifying separation from the comfortable parental world and its invasion of unknown life, and an image of a psychological experience which can occur whenever we have been clinging to naive, maidenlike views of life and are forced by experience to discover unknown depths in life and in ourselves.

INTRODUCTION

Myth portrays archetypal patterns in human life through pictures and stories. Greek myth is a sophisticated and perennially alive imaginative description of what we are made of inside. This is what seized the mind of the Renaissance, and it is what peeps from behind the often mystifying imagery of the Tarot cards, which transcend the changes in culture and consciousness of the last four millennia and restore us – like the old memory-systems – to a sense of connectedness with ancient and eternal designs.

We can now see that there are really two avenues by which to approach the Tarot cards. We can take the historical approach, which is essentially factual, or we can take the psychological approach, which is essentially archetypal. With the first we can explain – or can at least try to explain – the origins and initial intentions of the cards. But the second opens up the issue of their eternal fascination, despite the fact that we are more scientifically knowledgeable and now know better. In the imaginal world of the psyche, experiences are not connected by causality, but by meaning. Patterns other than the concrete ones are at work within us, and unless we have some understanding of the psyche, the strange coincidences of the Tarot cards can seem frightening or disturbing. Connections between events in outer life and the images of the Tarot cards are not because the cards are 'magical', but because there is a shared meaning. This is what we mean by birth, death and puberty being inner as well as outer experiences. We meet these experiences again and again on different levels at different times in life, and thus there is a Tarot card which will describe each of them, and which will somehow, mysteriously, appear without apparent 'cause' in a spread of cards at the moment when we are, inwardly, experiencing such an archetypal event. Thus the way in which the Tarot 'works' in a predictive sense is as a kind of mirror of the psyche. The archetypal nature of the images strikes hidden, unconscious chords in the card-reader, and reflects hitherto unknown knowledge or insight in relation to the client's situation – thus apparently revealing things which could not possibly, in any rational way, be discoverable. This is why 'clairvoyant' or 'psychic' powers are not a prerequisite for a sensitive reader, but rather, an awareness of the archetypal patterns or currents at

INTRODUCTION

work in life reflected by the images on the cards.

We may now turn to the cards themselves, to understand better the grand archetypal design, story or myth which is portrayed in their ancient images.

THE MAJOR ARCANA

The twenty-two cards which are called the Major Arcana of the Tarot are a series of images which portray the different stages of a journey. This journey is one which is familiar from many myths, legends and fairy tales, as well as from the world's great religious teachings. It is the journey of life which all human beings must make, from birth through childhood and the power and influence of the parents, through adolescence with its loves and conflicts and rebellions, through maturity with its worldly trials and ethical and moral challenges, through loss and crisis, despair and transformation and the awakening of new hope, toward eventual victory and achievement of the goal – which in turn leads to yet another journey. This cycle is not only a cycle of chronological age, but also a cycle which occurs many times within one life, for everything that happens to us has a beginning, a middle and an end. Thus the journey portrayed by the Major Arcana is archetypal, meaning that no matter what the specific details of an individual life might be, long or short, banal or dramatic, good or evil, certain stages of psychological development await us all. We have all been children and have all had parents; and we all continue to have a part of us which is childlike and ready to begin again. We have all experienced failures and triumphs, great or small, and we all grow, albeit sometimes unwillingly. Thus the archetypal journey of life, which is really an inner journey and occurs on many different levels, can be found in so many creative outpourings over the millennia. The ancient Babylonian epic *Gilgamesh* with its hero who must battle the dark forces is not really very different from the modern film *Star Wars*.

Inner changes precipitate external events, and external events foster inner changes. It is sometimes hard to say whether, for example, a love affair has caused a burst of creative activity and new insight, or whether new insights and a more creative way of looking at life have drawn us into a love affair. It is difficult to tell, also, whether a business failure instils bitterness and suspicion of others, or whether an innate suspicion and mistrust precipitates a business failure through alienation of colleagues. Thus the images of the Major Arcana describe both the inner state of the individual at a particular point in life, and the kind of

THE MAJOR ARCANA

THE MAJOR ARCANA

experiences the individual is likely to encounter in outer life. Inner and outer go together because the same individual is at the core of both. As the great Swiss psychiatrist Carl Jung once wrote, a person's life is characteristic of the person. Divination and psychological insight go hand in hand with the images of the Major Arcana, because what is happening outside us is linked to what is happening inside us. The mystery of why a particular Tarot card should appear in a spread as if 'by chance' yet eerily relevant not only to the psychological condition of the 'querent' (the person asking the question) but also to his or her circumstances at that moment, is inexplicable in ordinary causal terms. For this reason many people are frightened of the cards and believe they are in some way magical or supernatural. But they are no more so than the human psyche, which contains depths we know little about and which appears to be connected with the 'outer' world through cords of meaning. In some ways, understanding the inner meaning of a particular experience – What does this have to do with me? – can help us to cope better with that experience and respond to it in a richer and more creative way, because it no longer feels like chance or bad luck or blind fate. We can see the traces of our own characters in everything that happens to us.

The journey of the Major Arcana is really the journey of the Fool, who is the first of the twenty-two images. We follow the Fool, and in some profound sense also are the Fool, as he emerges from the darkness of the maternal cave and leaps out into the unknown. We meet the fundamental experiences of childhood – the worldly parents and the inner parents of the spirit and the imagination – in the cards of the Magician, the Empress, the Emperor, the High Priestess and the Hierophant. We recognize the conflicts and passions of the adolescent within us in the cards of the Lovers and the Chariot. We encounter the worldly tests and moral challenges of life in the cards of Justice, Temperance, Strength and the Hermit. We pass through crisis and loss and the sudden blow of fate portrayed by the Wheel of Fortune, and suffer the helplessness and despair of the Hanged Man and Death. We follow the Fool into confrontation with himself as the secret architect of his own fate in the Devil and the Tower. From this darkness hope is

THE MAJOR ARCANA

born in the cards of the Star, the Moon and the Sun; and victory over darkness and reconciliation with life come with the cards of Judgement and the World.

The images of the Major Arcana are ancient and evocative symbols of life experiences which belong to our human condition and our human destiny. Symbols such as these lend dignity to life, because we discover that others have been there before us, and have found a way through, and have grown and been enriched. All the cards have ambivalent meanings so they can suggest both positive and negative dimensions of experience. No card among the twenty-two is wholly 'good' or wholly 'bad', although some are easier or more difficult in terms of the quality of experience they portray. This is why we do not use the method of reversing the cards (interpreting them as 'good' if they appear the right way up in a spread, and as 'bad' if they appear upside down). This technique of reversals is a relatively modern innovation, and it can confuse rather than elucidate the meaning of the card. The 'weight' of a card for good or ill becomes more understandable in context of the overall pattern of the spread, which we will discuss more fully in the appropriate chapter. But an archetypal experience, and therefore the archetypal image which embodies it, is such a subtle intermingling of positive and negative that it is impossible to separate one fully from the other.

All the cards of the Major Arcana are rites of passage – stages or processes, rather than end results or static places which do not change. Every stage of life leads to the next one, and although we may understandably attempt to hold back time and remain in one comfortable place, it is not within our power as mortals to turn the moving cycle of life into a stagnant hiding-place. Thus at the end of the journey, the Fool begins again, because whenever we feel we have reached the goal and achieved our designs, another, deeper or higher goal materializes beyond it, so that every end is really a preparation for something else, and we begin the cycle again.

Now let us examine each of the twenty-two cards of the Major Arcana in more detail.

THE FOOL

The card of the Fool, the first of the Major Arcana, portrays a wild youth, dressed in ragged animal skins of different colours, dancing in ecstatic abandonment at the edge of a precipice. He wears a wreath of vine leaves in his chestnut hair, and bears little horns, like those of a goat, on his brow. His eyes are raised to the dawn breaking in the distance, where the sun can just be seen above the horizon. Around him lies a formidable barren landscape of brown and grey rocks. To his left, hidden in the shadows of the receding night, is the mouth of the cave from which he has emerged. Above it, on a bare branch, perches an eagle.

The eagle is the bird of Zeus, king of the gods, who watches over the Fool as he prepares to plunge into the unknown.

The cave from which the Fool emerges is the past, the dark and undifferentiated mass from which the beginning of a true sense of individuality is about to take form.

The goat's horns on the Fool's brow suggest, like the animal skins he wears, that he is like a young animal, driven into life by instinct, not yet conscious or possessed of understanding.

Here we meet the hero of our journey in the guise of the mysterious god Dionysos, the Twice-Born. He was the child of great Zeus, king of the gods, and Semele, a mortal woman and a princess of Thebes. Zeus' wife Hera, furious at his infidelity, disguised herself as a nursemaid and whispered to Semele that she must test her lover's devotion by demanding that he appear before her in all his divine glory. Having promised Semele anything her heart might desire, the god was bound by his vow when she insisted that he reveal his divinity to her. Reluctantly, he manifested as thunder and lightning, and Semele was consumed in flames. But Zeus managed

THE FOOL

to rescue the unborn child. Hermes, messenger of the gods and patron of magic, sewed up the foetus in Zeus' thigh; thus Dionysos was born.

Hera continued to pursue the strange horned child, and sent the Titans, the earth-gods, to tear Dionysos to pieces. But Zeus rescued the child's heart, still beating. This heart he transformed into a potion of pomegranate seeds, and the magical drink was fed to the maiden Persephone by Hades, the dark god of the underworld, when he abducted her. Persephone became pregnant, and Dionysos was thus reborn in the underworld. Therefore he was called Dionysos-Iacchos, the Twice-Born, god of light and ecstasy. Ordained by his father Zeus to live among men and share their suffering, he was stricken with madness by Hera, and wandered all over the world followed by wild satyrs, madwomen and animals. He gave the gift of wine to mankind, and brought drunken ecstasy and spiritual redemption to those who were willing to relinquish their attachment to worldly power and wealth. Eventually his heavenly father Zeus bade him rise to Olympus, where he took his place at the right hand of the king of the gods.

On an inner level, Dionysos, the Fool, is an image of the mysterious impulse within us to leap into the unknown. The conservative, cautious, realistic side of us watches with horror this wild, youthful spirit who, trusting in heaven, is prepared to walk over the cliff's edge without a moment's hesitation. The madness of Dionysos seems mad only to that part of us which is bound to the world of form, facts and logical order. But in a more profound sense it is not madness, for it is the impulse toward change which comes upon us 'out of the blue', which has no rational basis and no preplanned programme of action. The god is portrayed in animal skins because, in a way, this intuitive, irrational dimension to the human personality is a kind of sixth sense, an animal instinct which hears a music to which jaded ears, used to concrete reality, are not attuned. Dionysos is the son of the king of the gods, and it is his father's spirit to which he is in tune, although he is ordained to live on earth with mortals; but it is difficult to know, when this impulse strikes us, whether it has come from Zeus' heavenly abode or a darker, more underworld place.

THE FOOL

Thus Dionysos, the Fool, represents the irrational impulse toward change and toward opening life's horizons into the unknown. The Fool stands at the beginning of his journey, and when we are struck by the mysterious impulse which he represents, we too stand at the threshold of a journey. These irrational impulses can sometimes be destructive, and sometimes creative; and often they are both together. The wild god can sometimes leap off the cliff's edge into painful and damaging situations which may also yield wonderfully creative beginnings, and so can the individual who is overwhelmed by the strange inexplicable craving for some spiritual food which he or she cannot fully understand. But if we never respond to these calls from the other world, then we sink into drab, meaningless, banal lives, and wonder, at the end of life, what we have missed and why the world seems so empty. Thus the Fool is a highly ambivalent figure, for there is no guarantee at the beginning of such a journey whether we will arrive safely, if at all. Yet not to begin is to deny the god, which on an inner level means to deny all in us that is youthful, creative, and in touch with that which is greater than ourselves.

On a divinatory level, Dionysos, the Fool, augurs the advent of a new chapter of life when he appears in a spread. A risk of some kind is required, a willingness to jump out into the unknown. The Fool is ambiguous just as Dionysos is, for we cannot know whether we will enter the Fool's perception of the divine or end up merely looking foolish. In this way, amidst ambiguity and excitement and fear, begins the great journey of life portrayed by the Major Arcana of the Tarot.

THE MAGICIAN

The card of the Magician portrays a wiry, slender young man with curling black hair, who stands facing us at a crossroads. He is dressed for the road in a short white tunic and a deep red travelling cloak. With his left hand he points upward toward heaven. With the right he gestures at a flat rock which lies before him at the centre of the convergence of roads. On the rock four objects are assembled: a chalice, a sword, a flaming wand or caduceus entwined by two snakes, and a pentacle. Behind him can be seen a barren landscape of brown and grey rocks – a continuation of the landscape which we met in the card of the Fool. Two branches of the road vanish in the rocky distance.

The cup represents the Cup of Fortune, particularly fortune in love, for Hermes is wise in the knowledge of the heart.

The sword represents the cutting edge of the mind and its power, given to Hermes by his father Zeus.

The bag of pentacles or coins marks Hermes as the god of sudden good luck and as the patron of merchants and businessmen.

The caduceus is Hermes' wand of magic, entwined by two snakes which represent all opposites: good and evil, male and female, dark and light.

Here we meet the god Hermes, guide of travellers, patron of thieves and liars, ruler of magic and divination, and bringer of sudden good luck and changes in fortune. He is called the Trickster because he is deceitful and ambiguous, yet he is the trusted messenger of the gods and the guide of souls into the underworld. In Greek myth Hermes was the son of Zeus, king of the gods, and the mysterious nymph Maia, who is also called Mother Night. Thus he is the child of both spiritual light and primordial darkness, and his colours – red and white – reflect the mixture of earthly passions and

THE MAGICIAN

spiritual clarity which are part of his nature.

When Hermes was only a baby he toddled out of his cradle and stole a herd of cattle from his brother Apollo, the sun-god. To fool Apollo he put on sandals which faced backward, so that the angry god went in the wrong direction looking for the culprit. When Apollo finally confronted him about who had stolen his cattle, Hermes presented him with a gift: a lyre which he made from a tortoiseshell. Hermes flattered his brother with praise from a wily, honeyed tongue, telling the older god that the gift was meant to honour Apollo's wonderful skill at music. Apollo was so beguiled that he forgot about the cattle, and in return bestowed upon Hermes a gift of his own: that of divination. Hermes thus became the master of the four elements, and eventually taught men the skills of geomancy (divination by earth), pyromancy (divination by fire), hydromancy (divination by water), and aeromancy (divination by air). He was always worshipped at crossroads, where statues called Herms were erected to honour him and invoke his blessings upon the traveller, the wanderer and the homeless.

On an inner level, Hermes, the Magician, is the guide. This means that somewhere within us, no matter how lost or confused we might be at any point in life, there is something within which has foresight and resources which are often hidden from consciousness but which can divine what direction to take and what choices to make. The Magician does not come when he is called, for Hermes is a wily and playful god, and does not always respond to what we think is an important situation. He has his own ideas of what might be important. He comes in the night, often in the form of disturbing dreams, or in the guise of a meeting with another person who turns out to be somehow significant as a catalyst on the journey. Or Hermes can appear as a sudden hunch, or the discovery that one knows more than one thought. The book which one 'accidentally' reads, or the chance visit from a friend, or any of a thousand strange little 'turns of fate', are the handiwork of the Magician, the inner guide. In a sense the Magician is spiritual teacher and protector of the Fool, just as in the myth the god Hermes managed to sew the unborn Dionysos into Zeus' thigh and looked after the child

THE MAGICIAN

until he was born. Hermes, the Magician, is that unconscious power within which looks after us although we cannot see him, and which appears as though by magic at the most critical and difficult moments in life to offer guidance and wisdom.

Hermes was not a god upon whom one could rely for the ordinary decisions of everyday life. He could be tricky and treacherous, and often his directions led men and women astray into the night, through convoluted paths that left the known and well-trodden landscape and took the traveller into strange and frustrating places. To follow the inner guide does not always mean making the choices which are secure and guarantee results. Often they are the opposite. But because Hermes is the master of the four elements, his wisdom can penetrate all the spheres of life – the mind, the imagination, the heart and the body. Without him we have no inner resources at all, but must always rely upon the direction of others, and are doomed to travel like sheep on the same worn track as everybody else. The Fool meets the Magician only after he has braved the precipice, for the visitations of the inner guide do not come when one hides safely within the maternal cave.

On a divinatory level, Hermes, the Magician, points to potential skills and creative abilities which have not yet manifested. He may appear as an upsurge of energy and an intuition of exciting new opportunities. He presages insight and an awareness of unexplored possibilities. The Fool is blind, with only his animal sense of a meaning to be found somewhere, somehow. But through his meeting with Hermes, the Magician, it becomes clear that the journey is possible, and that one has capacities that have yet to be developed.

THE EMPRESS

The card of the Empress portrays a beautiful earthy woman with rich flowing brown hair, obviously pregnant and standing in a field of ripening barley. Her gown is woven of many different plants, and hemmed with leafy boughs. Around her neck is a necklace of twelve precious stones. She is crowned with a diadem of castles and towers. Behind her, in a background of fertile fields, water flows into a pool.

The waterfall suggests the flow of feeling and fertility of Demeter's world. She presides over the rites of marriage and blesses the fruits of its union.

The diadem of castles and towers which Demeter wears represents her rulership over the instinct to build secure homes in stone and wood, places of safety and peace.

The necklace of twelve stones symbolizes the twelve signs of the zodiac. As ruler of nature, Demeter governs the orderly cycle of the seasons and the laws of the cosmos.

Here we meet the great goddess Demeter, who is Earth Mother, ruler of all nature and protectress of young defenseless creatures. In Greek myth, Demeter ripened the golden grain each year, and in late summer the people offered thanks to her for the bounty of the earth. Demeter governed the orderly cycles of nature and the life of all growing things – hence the gown in which she is clothed. She presided over the gestation and birth of new life, and blessed the rites of marriage as a vessel for the continuity of nature. Demeter is a matriarchal goddess, an image of the power within the earth itself, which needs no spiritual validation from heaven. She was said to have taught men the arts of ploughing and tilling the soil, and women the arts of grinding wheat and baking bread.

Demeter lived with her daughter Persephone sheltered from the

THE EMPRESS

conflicts and quarrels of the world. But one day this peaceful, happy life was violently changed. Persephone had gone out walking and did not return. In anguish Demeter searched everywhere for her daughter, but Persephone had vanished without trace. Eventually, after years of hopeless wandering, word came of Persephone's fate. It seemed that Hades, the dark lord of the underworld, had been overcome with desire for the maiden, and had risen out of the earth in his chariot drawn by two black horses and abducted her.

Demeter in her rage allowed the earth to fall barren, and refused to restore it to its former abundance. Because she could not accept the change which had occurred – even though Persephone had willingly eaten of the pomegranate, the fruit of the underworld, and Hades had treated her with honour and made her his queen – it seemed as if the whole of mankind would perish from lack of food. Eventually, thanks to the intercession of the clever and all-seeing god Hermes, a compromise was agreed upon. For nine months of the year, Persephone would live with her mother, but for the remaining three she must return to her dark husband.

Demeter never came to terms with this solution. Every year while her daughter was away, the Earth Mother went into mourning. Flowers withered, trees shed their leaves, and the earth grew lifeless and cold. But every year, on Persephone's return, the spring came again.

On an inner level, the image of Demeter, the Empress, reflects the experience of mothering. This does not mean only the physical processes of gestation, birth and nurturing of the young and helpless child. It is also the inner experience of the Great Mother: the discovery of the body as something valuable and precious which merits care, the experience of being part of nature and rooted in natural life, the appreciation of the senses and the simple pleasures of daily existence. Without this Great Mother within us, we can bring nothing to fruition, for this is the side of us which has the patience and gentleness to wait until the time is ripe for action. Without her we cannot appreciate our physical selves, but live disconnected in a purely intellectual world without any grounding or respect for reality. A child's experience of

THE EMPRESS

Mother is connected with the feeling of safety and trust in life, and the image of the Empress is likewise connected with the inner feeling of security and safety in the present. She is wise, but not in a cerebral way. Hers is the wisdom of nature, which understands that all things move in cycles and ripen at the appropriate time.

But like all the images in the Tarot deck, Demeter has her dark side. Nothing but nature means stagnation of the spirit, and an apathy and dullness which crush all possibility of change. Demeter is not only the Good Mother; she is also the Mourning Mother, who cannot relinquish her possessions and who avenges any intrusion of life's conflicts into her ordered, Eden-like world. This Mourning Mother can be full of bitterness and resentment because life requires change and separation, and endings must occur. Thus when the Fool on his archetypal journey encounters Demeter, the Empress, he is thrust into the dark and light dimensions of his own instinctual nature.

On a divinatory level, the appearance of the Empress in a spread suggests the onset of a more earthy phase of life. A marriage or the birth of a child might occur; or the birth of a creative child, an artistic offspring, for this too requires the patience and nurturing of the Great Mother. Through this card we enter the realm of the body and the instincts, as a place of both peace and stagnation, life-giving and life-suffocating. Thus the Fool, the child of heaven, discovers that he lives in a physical body and is a creature not only of spirit but also of earth.

THE EMPEROR

The card of the Emperor portrays a mature man with broad and muscular shoulders and chest. His rich, flowing hair and beard are vivid auburn, and his eyes are a clear sky-blue. He faces us seated on a golden throne at the top of a mountain. His robe is purple bordered with gold, and on his head is a golden crown. In his right hand he holds three lightning bolts; in his left rests the globe of the world. An eagle perches on his shoulder. Behind him stretches a backdrop of snow-capped peaks.

The lightning bolt is Zeus' symbol of power not only because of its awesome grandeur, but also because it lights up the sky. Zeus is a god of inspiration and sudden creative vision, and the lightning symbolizes his revelation of the truth.

Zeus made his abode the mountain peaks because he is a god of mental and spiritual heights, and his will rises above the bondage of the body and the limitations of nature.

The eagle is Zeus' emblem because of its keen sight and power to fly higher than other birds. As a bird of prey, it also expresses the aggression and conquering instinct of the god.

Here we meet great Zeus, king of the gods, whom the Greeks called All-Father, creator of the world and sovereign of both gods and men. In myth, Zeus was the youngest son of the Titans Cronos and Rhea. A prophecy was given to Cronos that one day one of his sons would overthrow him and take his place. To guard against this, he decided to destroy his children, and for five years running, as Rhea bore him sons and daughters, he snatched them from her arms and swallowed them before they opened their eyes.

This naturally did not please Rhea, who when she knew that a sixth child was to be born fled secretly to Arcadia and gave birth to Zeus in a cave. Then she wrapped a large stone in swaddling clothes and presented it to Cronos as her son. He promptly swallowed it. In time

THE EMPEROR

Zeus grew to manhood, and came to Cronos disguised as a cupbearer. He prepared a potion for his father which made him violently sick, and out of the old god's mouth came all the five children he had swallowed, quite unharmed. Out, too, came the stone. Zeus then led his brothers and sisters in rebellion against Cronos and overthrew him, and inaugurated a new rule.

The new king of the gods made the mountain of Olympus his home, and established a hierarchy of gods who obeyed his ultimate law. His symbols of power were the thunder and the lightning bolt. His volatile, fiery, profligate spirit expressed itself not only in the thunderstorm, but also in the many lovers whom he pursued and the many children whom he fathered. Among them were Athene (goddess of justice), Dike (goddess of natural law), Moira (goddess of fate), and the nine Muses (patrons of the arts). His wife was Hera, goddess of marriage and childbirth, who ruled as his consort. Zeus dispensed good and evil according to the laws which he established. He was also god of the hearth and of friendship, and the protector of all men.

On an inner level, Zeus, the Emperor, is an image of the experience of fathering. It is the father who embodies our spiritual ideals, our ethical codes, the self-sufficiency with which we survive in the world, the authority and ambition which drive us to achieve, and the discipline and foresight necessary to accomplish our goals. This masculine principle within both men and women differs from the nurturing and unconditional love of the mother whom we met in the card of the Empress. Here it is the spirit, not the body, which is accorded the highest value, and action, rather than intuitive flowing with nature, which is demanded of us.

The father within us also fosters self-respect, because it is this part of us which can take a standpoint from which to meet life's challenges. Zeus could be compassionate, and championed the weak and the dispossessed. But he could also be angry and vindictive if his authority was challenged and his laws broken. Thus Zeus, the Emperor, has a darker face, which is expressed on an inner level as rigidity and implacable self-righteousness. To be in relationship with the inner

THE EMPEROR

father means to possess a sense of one's potency, one's capacity to initiate ideas and concretize them in the world. To be dominated by the inner father means to be enslaved by a set of beliefs which crush all human feeling with their inflexibility and arrogance. Then, like Zeus himself, we must overthrow the old rule and inaugurate a newer and more creative one, lest we become petty tyrants ourselves or fall under the spell of a tyrant in the world outside. Having discovered the rich and fecund world of the body's needs and pleasures, the Fool must now find ethical principles by which to live; for without the Emperor, we are mere pawns in life, driven from within and without by blind instinct, blaming our problems and difficulties on other people and on society, because we cannot find the inner experience of strength which the father embodies.

On a divinatory level, Zeus, the Emperor, augurs a confrontation with the issue of the father principle in both its positive and negative forms. We are challenged to make something manifest, to concretize a creative idea, to build something in the world, to found a business perhaps, or to establish the structure of a home and family. We are asked to take a standpoint, to become effective and powerful, to formulate our ideas and ethics. We are also asked to consider where the creative young king has become the rigid, oppressive tyrant, and where our idealogies are interfering with life and growth. When the Fool meets the Emperor after his sojourn in the instinctual world, he learns to confront worldly life with his own resources, alone, according to ethics which he must develop for himself. Then he can progress on his journey with the certainty that he can be effective in life because there is something higher in which he believes, and whose authority he himself now embodies.

THE HIGH PRIESTESS

The card of the High Priestess portrays a slender, ethereal young woman with pale skin, long black hair and dark eyes, dressed in a simple white gown. On her head is a golden crown. In her right hand she holds a pomegranate, split open to show its multitude of seeds. In her left hand a bunch of white narcissi trail to the ground. On either side of the stairway on which she stands is a pillar; the left one is black, the right one white. Behind her, at the top of the staircase, a doorway opens out on to the rich green landscape which appears in the card of the Empress.

The pomegranate is both the fruit of the dead and of conjugal love because of its many seeds. Thus Persephone's hidden world is fertile and full of undeveloped creative potential.

The black and white pillars reflect the duality contained in the underworld. Both creative potentials and destructive impulses are hidden in the darkness of the unconscious.

The narcissus, which Persephone picked when Hades abducted her, was associated with the dead because of its ghostly colour and its annual emergence from the winter earth.

Here we meet Persephone, queen of the underworld, daughter of the Earth Mother Demeter and guardian of the secrets of the dead. We have already seen, in the card of the Empress, how, according to the myth, Hades, lord of the underworld, was overwhelmed with desire for the maiden while she wandered in the fields picking flowers, and rose up out of the earth to abduct her. When he had brought her to his dark abode, he offered her a pomegranate, which she ate. Having partaken of the fruit of the dead, she was thus bound to him forever.

Persephone ruled over the underworld with her husband for three months of the year. Although the remaining nine months were spent in

THE HIGH PRIESTESS

the daylight world with her mother Demeter, she could never speak of the secrets she had learned in the land of the dead. The realm of Hades, full of mysteries and riches, was ringed round by the terrible river Styx, over which no living man or woman could cross without the permission of Hades himself; although Hermes, messenger of the gods and guide of souls, could usher through those exceptional heroes who had gained the god's consent. Even the souls of the dead could not cross without paying a coin to Charon, the old ferryman who rowed the boat of passage across the Styx, for at the gateway to Hades' realm crouched the terrifying three-headed dog Cerberus who devoured any trespasser, living or dead, who did not respect the laws of the invisible realm. Thus, through eating the pomegranate, Persephone left behind her innocent girlhood, and became the guardian of this shadowy realm and custodian of its secrets.

On an inner level, Persephone, the High Priestess, is an image of the link with that mysterious inner world to which depth psychology has given the name 'the unconscious'. It is as though, beneath and beyond the ordinary daylight world which we believe to be reality, lies another, hidden world, full of riches and potentials, which we cannot penetrate without the consent of its invisible rulers. This world contains our undeveloped potentials as well as the darker, more primitive facets of the personality. It also holds the secret of the destiny of the individual, which gestates in darkness until the time is ripe for manifestation. Persephone, the High Priestess, is an embodiment of that part of us which knows the secrets of the inner world. But she can only be dimly sensed by waking consciousness, and appears through the fleeting fragments of dreams, or through those strange coincidences which make us begin to wonder whether there might be some hidden pattern at work in our lives.

Persephone is a seductive and fascinating figure, but she does not speak of her secrets. In the same way the night-world of the unconscious, glimpsed through dreams and fantasies and intuitions, is also seductive and fascinating, but when we try to grasp it with the intellect and 'master' it for our own purposes, it remains mute and

THE HIGH PRIESTESS

slides away. The dark world of Persephone provides only shadowy glimpses of patterns and movements at work within the individual, which require patience and the passage of time before they can be brought into the light of day. The myth of Persephone emphasizes the cyclical motion of time, portraying a mysterious rhythm, a constant coming and going of something. The seeds of change and new potentials wait silently in the womb of the underworld before they are given over to the care of the Earth Mother and brought to birth in the material world. Persephone, the High Priestess, is an image of that natural law at work within the depths of the soul which governs the unfoldment of destiny from an invisible source, and which is revealed only through feeling, intuition and the night-world of dreams.

On a divinatory level, the appearance of the High Priestess in a spread augurs the heightening of the powers of intuition, and implies that there will be an encounter of some kind with the hidden inner world which Persephone rules. The individual may be drawn inexplicably to this world through an interest in the occult or the esoteric, or through the effects of a powerful dream or the uncanny sense that 'something' is at work in one's life. Thus the Fool, having learned something of his physical nature and needs and his place in the world through his earthly parents, the Empress and the Emperor, now enters the night-world, and comes, often with confusion and bewilderment, to that silent figure who embodies Mother on another, deeper and subtler level – the womb of the unconscious in which the secret of his real purpose and the pattern of his destiny are contained.

THE HIEROPHANT

The card of the Hierophant portrays a strange figure, a Centaur, with the torso, arms and head of a man and the body of a horse. His long brown hair and beard and his benign, mature face suggest a priest or a teacher. In his left hand he holds a scroll containing written wisdom. His right hand is held up in an ancient sign of blessing. To either side of him is a stone pillar. Behind him can be seen the rough rock of the cave which is both his home and his temple. Light streams down upon his crowned head from a circular opening in the roof of the cave.

The cave which is Chiron's temple is a natural earthy formation, not a man-made place of worship, for it is only through applying spiritual teaching in ordinary physical life that it can be rendered valid.

The twin pillars are the pillars of the hall of knowledge through which the disciple enters to receive Chiron's teaching.

The scroll which the Centaur carries is the scroll of the law, the written word which through revelation communicates the will of the divine.

Here we meet Chiron, king of the Centaurs, healer, priest and wise teacher of all the young heroes in myth. Chiron's birth was itself very mysterious, for he was born of the union of Ixion, son of the war-god Ares, and a cloud which Zeus fashioned in the likeness of his wife Hera in order to prevent Ixion from making love to the goddess herself. The Centaur was educated by Apollo the sun-god and Artemis the moon-goddess, and because of his great wisdom and spirituality was made king of the Centaurs and given the task of instilling into the young Greek princes of noble houses the spiritual values and respect for divine law which they needed even before they learned the arts of rulership and feats of arms.

THE HIEROPHANT

Chiron was also a great healer, and knew the secrets of herbs and plant lore. But he was unable to heal himself. One day his friend, the hero Heracles, visited him in his cave after the hero had killed the monstrous Hydra with its nine poisonous heads. Heracles accidentally grazed the Centaur in the thigh with one of the arrows that had been dipped in the blood of the monster. This blood was deadly poison, and no matter what Chiron did he could not draw the posion from the wound. Because he was immortal, he could not die, and was thus condemned to live in pain, sacrificing all worldly happiness and devoting his time to the teaching of spiritual wisdom.

On an inner level, Chiron, the Hierophant, is an image of that part of us which reaches upward toward the spirit in order to understand what is required of us by God. He is the inner spiritual teacher, the priest who establishes a link between ordinary worldly consciousness and intuitive knowledge of God's law. While the world of Persephone, the High Priestess, is dark and elusive, and cannot be comprehended by the intellect, the world of Chiron can be elucidated and interpreted by the mind. The ancient word for priest, *pontifex*, means 'maker of bridges', for the role of the priest both within and outside us is to serve as a spiritual father, establishing a relationship between man and God and making clear the nature of the laws by which we must live in order to be in right relationship with the divine. The Emperor's laws, embodying the father principle on earth, are concerned with right behaviour in the world. But the laws of the Hierophant are concerned with right behaviour in the eyes of God. But Chiron does not symbolize any orthodox religious system. He is a wild creature, half man and half animal, and his temple is not man-made but rather a cave within a mountain. Thus the spiritual law which he transmits is not a collective one distilled into dogma, but an individual one which can be found only by relationship with the priest within. Thus different people experience God differently, and we come to our own spiritual understanding according to our own particular relationship with what 'God' might really mean.

Chiron's injury makes him the Wounded Healer, the one who through his own pain can understand and appreciate the pain of others

THE HIEROPHANT

and can therefore see further and higher than those who are merely blindly content. Thus Chiron, the Hierophant, represents a wounded part of ourselves, where some unsolvable problem or limitation deepens us and makes us compassionate where otherwise we would be merely shallow and mouth platitudes of goodness without any real sense of what it might mean. The true priest is open to the world's pain and longing because he himself suffers. The image of Chiron relates us to the value of those insurmountable limitations or wounds within us, which although they may cause suffering in ordinary life, nevertheless make us question and open the way to a greater understanding of the higher laws of life. This paradox is also suggested by the Centaur himself, for being half god and half horse he partakes both of the instincts and of the spirit, and contains a duality which is part of our human condition. We are neither wholly beast nor wholly divine, but a mixture of both, and must learn to live with both. Out of this mixture comes the wisdom of the Centaur, which partakes both of the knowledge of God and the knowledge of natural law – God manifesting in the world of form.

On a divinatory level, Chiron, the Hierophant, implies when he appears in a spread that the individual will begin to actively seek answers of a philosophical kind. This may emerge as the study of a particular philosophy or system of belief, or as a deep commitment to a quest for meaning in life. The Hierophant may appear in the form of an analyst, psychotherapist, priest or spiritual mentor in outside life to whom we turn for comfort and help. The Fool thus emerges from his discovery of the underworld and the hidden powers of the unconscious seeking answers to the enigma of himself and the meaning of his life. When he meets the Hierophant he encounters that part of himself which can begin to formulate and express a personal philosophy, an individual vision of the spirit, which guides him as he leaves his childhood behind and ventures out into life's challenges.

THE LOVERS

The card of the Lovers portrays a handsome, fresh-faced blonde youth, dressed in simple shepherd's garb and holding a crook in his right hand. In his left hand he holds a golden apple. Three women parade themselves before him, for this is a beauty contest, and the golden apple will be awarded to the winner. The woman on the left is regal and mature, with vivid auburn hair and blue eyes, robed in imperial purple and wearing a golden diadem. She offers the young man the globe of the world. The woman in the centre is young, seductive and black-haired. Her diaphanous rose-coloured robe reveals more than it conceals. She offers a golden cup. The woman on the right is cool and chaste, dressed in full battle armour; her pale hair is half-hidden by a warrior's helmet. She offers a sword. Behind the four figures stretches an undulating landscape of lush green hills.

The goddess Hera, spouse and mouthpiece of Zeus, offers the globe of the world which represents the worldly authority and ethical perspective of Zeus, the Emperor.

Athene offers a sword, which we will meet later in the Suit of Swords, and which symbolizes the cutting power of the mind and the keen vision and decisiveness which belong to the mental realm.

The goddess Aphrodite offers the cup of love, which we will meet later in the Suit of Cups, and which is a symbol of relationship.

Here we meet the Trojan prince Paris, who was commanded by Zeus to judge a beauty contest between three goddesses – Hera, Aphrodite and Athene. When Paris was born, an oracle declared that one day he would be the downfall of his father's kingdom. His father, King Priam of Troy, sentenced him to death by exposure on a hillside, but he was rescued by a kind shepherd. Paris grew to manhood tending sheep, filling his spare hours with romantic conquests, for he was a very handsome and charming young man.

THE LOVERS

When a quarrel broke out on Mount Olympus between Hera (queen of the gods), Aphrodite (goddess of sensual love) and Athene (goddess of justice), as to who was the loveliest, Zeus decided that Paris, with his rich and varied experience of women, would be the best judge of the contest. Hermes was sent to inform the young man of this dubious honour accorded him by the king of the gods.

Paris understandably first refused the request, knowing full well that whichever goddess he chose, the other two would never forgive him. But Hermes threatened him with Zeus' ire. Paris then kindly offered to divide the apple in three, for how could he choose between three such radiant goddesses? But Hermes would not accept that excuse either. The goddesses then paraded before the young man. Hera offered him rulership of the world if he chose her. Athene offered to make him the mightiest and most just of warriors. Aphrodite simply opened her robes, and offered him the cup of love, and promised him the most beautiful mortal woman in the world as his bride.

The result was a foregone conclusion. Paris, being young and therefore not yet clear about his inner values, chose Aphrodite without hesitation. His reward was the famous Helen, queen of Sparta and, inconveniently, someone else's wife. Hera and Athene smiled and promised that they would not hold his choice against him, and then walked off arm in arm plotting the downfall of Troy. Thus started the conflagration of the Trojan War, which began with the anger of Helen's cuckolded husband and ended with the city being burned to the ground and all its royal house destroyed. And so the oracle proved true.

On an inner level, the Judgement of Paris, as it is known in myth, is an image of the first of life's great challenges to the developing individual: the problem of choice in love. This dilemma is not only about trying to decide between two women, or two men. It also reflects our values, because our choices mirror back to us the kind of person we wish to become. Paris, because of his youth and the driving force of his sexual needs, cannot truly choose from a mature perspective. His choice is made by his desires, rather than by himself. Here is the problem of free will versus the compulsions of the instincts.

THE LOVERS

The consequences of choices in love are enormous, for they affect all levels of life. The compulsive choice of Paris ultimately results in the great conflict of the Trojan War. It is not that he has made the 'wrong' choice, for he is not yet centred enough to balance the erotic attractions of Aphrodite against the result of stealing someone else's wife. Nor does he know himself well enough yet to ascertain whether worldly power or a warrior's leadership might be equally important to him. The contest is forced upon him, just as life forces such challenges upon all of us before we feel ready, and in a sense his 'mistake' is necessary and inevitable. Desire for another person forces the development of individual values and self-knowledge through the messes and conflicts which arise from one's choice. Such a situation cannot be avoided, because it is archetypal. Paris is an image of that side of us which, governed by the uncontained need for satisfaction of desire, cannot yet see that all choices have consequences for which we are ultimately responsible. Without passing through this initiation by fire, we cannot understand how we create our own futures, but instead blame the results on fate, chance, or someone else's fault, rather than our own lack of reflection.

On a divinatory level, the card of the Lovers when it appears in a spread augurs the necessity of a choice of some kind, usually in love. The Fool, having learned about his own duality, must now put his values to the test. Sometimes this means a love triangle, but it can also mean the problem of too hasty a marriage, or a choice between love and a career or some creative activity. This card implies the necessity of looking carefully at the implications of one's choices, rather than being driven blindly, thereby inaugurating, like Paris, a great conflagration.

THE CHARIOT

The card of the Chariot portrays a handsome, virile man with curling auburn hair, blue eyes and ruddy complexion, driving a bronze war-chariot. He is dressed in bronze armour, bronze helmet and a blood-red tunic. At his hip is a bronze shield, and at his side is balanced a large spear. He grips the reins of two horses, one black and one white, which pull in opposite directions before him. The dusty road on which he travels winds into a reddish, desert-like landscape, while the sky lowers with an impending storm.

The desert landscape through which Ares drives lacks water – an image of the lack of feeling and relatedness in which the aggressive impulses thrive. Yet Ares and Aphrodite are drawn together, as though the instincts of strife and relatedness are in some way secretly connected.

Ares' spear forms the traditonal symbol for the masculine – an image of phallic power and potency in both men and women.

The black and white horses, like the dual columns in the card of the High Priestess, reflect the potential for both good and evil contained in the aggressive instinct.

Here we meet the war-god Ares, who was said in myth to have been conceived by Hera, queen of the gods, without male seed. As god of war, Ares revelled in fighting. His two squires, Deimos (Fear) and Phobos (Terror) – sometimes said to be his sons – accompanied him on the battlefield. Unlike the goddess Athene, who as a war-deity represented cool strategy and foresight, Ares was in love with the heat and glory of battle itself, and with the exultant unleashing of his strength to challenge the foe.

Ares was in many ways an unappealing god because he was associated with conflict and bloodshed, and Olympian Zeus and Athene disliked him for his brute strength and lack of refinement. But the love-goddess Aphrodite had different tastes. Impressed by the vigour of the

THE CHARIOT

handsome warrior whom she doubtless compared with her ill-favoured husband, the smith-god Hephaistos, she fell in love with Ares. The sentiment was quickly reciprocated. Ares took unscrupulous advantage of Hephaistos' absence to dishonour the marital couch. But the husband discovered the adulterous affair, and planned a witty revenge. Secretly he forged a net so fine that it could not be seen, but so strong that it could not be broken. He arranged this net above the couch where the lovers normally frolicked. When next the couple met and later fell asleep, the invisible net spread over them, and Hephaistos called all the gods to witness the shame of his wife and her lover. But Ares' ardour was unquenched by his embarrassment, and later, from his union with Aphrodite, a daughter was born – Harmonia, whose quality, as her name suggests, was a harmonious balancing of love and strife.

On an inner level, Ares, the driver of the Chariot, is an image of the aggressive instincts guided and directed by the will of consciousness. The horses which pull the Chariot in opposite directions are portrayals of the conflicting animal urges within ourselves, full of vitality yet unwilling to work in harmony. They must be handled with strength and firmness, yet not repressed or broken, or we lose the power and potency to survive and make our way in life. Ares, the fatherless god, is in some ways an image of the natural aggressive and competitive instincts of the body itself, for he lacks the archetypal spiritual father who might provide him with vision and meaning. But his iron will and great courage are a necessary dimension of human character, for spiritual vision alone is not sufficient to survive in a competitive, difficult world.

Having invoked conflict as a result of his choices in love, the Fool must now confront the second of life's great lessons: the creative harnessing of the violent, turbulent urges of the instinctual nature. Thus, through the figure of Ares, the driver of the Chariot, he arrives at maturity. In the card of the Lovers, the Fool is still an adolescent, compelled by romantic dreams and the desire to possess a beautiful object. But through the Chariot he learns to take the consequences of his actions like a man, and faces the anger and conflict which he has

THE CHARIOT

invoked both inside and outside himself. Like the Fool, we – men and women both – must learn to struggle with the warring opposites and warlike urges within ourselves, if we are to survive in the jungle of life. In myth, Ares is forever getting into trouble, either through an angry quarrel with someone or through the ruthless pursuit of a love-object. But he survives all his humiliations and defeats, and emerges stronger. Ultimately he fathers a child who embodies the serenity which can be found at the end of a conflict which has been creatively handled. The strife which Ares embodies is a necessary experience. No matter how spiritually committed or selflessly loving we attempt to become, the aggressive drives within us do not die. They can be disowned and forced into the unconscious, where they re-emerge as illness or are projected upon others who then unleash aggression upon us. But if we can meet the challenge of Ares, then we can be more honest about this vital force within, and the struggle of learning to contain and direct it fosters development of the whole personality.

On a divinatory level, the card of the Chariot appearing in a spread augurs conflict and struggle which can result in a stronger personality. One may come face to face not only with aggression in others, but with one's own competitive and aggressive drives. This conflict cannot be avoided, but needs to be faced with strength and containment. Thus the Fool comes to harmony through learning to handle his own contradictions, and passes from the world of adolescence to the next stage of his journey.

JUSTICE

The card of Justice portrays a severely beautiful young woman, dressed in silver helmet and battle armour, seated on a silver throne. In her right hand she holds an upright sword. In her left she holds a pair of scales. Her pale hair and white robes echo the purity of the two white columns and portico which frame her. Beneath her feet is a floor patterned of black and white marble. An owl perches on her left shoulder.

The black and white patterned floor suggests the mind's capacity to integrate both dark and light into an orderly and coherent design.

The owl, Athene's bird, reflects her clarity of vision, because it can see and hunt its prey in the dark.

The scales symbolize the capacity to weigh one thing against another to arrive at an impartial judgement. In myth, Athene was said to have invented the first human jury.

Here we meet Athene, goddess of Justice, whom we earlier encountered in the card of the Lovers. In myth, her father was Zeus, king of the gods, who had been warned by Uranus that if he had a child by his first wife, Metis, goddess of Wisdom, it would be more powerful than he. To forestall this eventuality he swallowed Metis before she had given birth to the child she was carrying. Shortly afterward, Zeus was tormented by an intolerable headache. To cure him, Hephaistos, the smith-god, split open his head with a bronze axe, and from the gaping wound sprang the fully armed Athene, shouting a triumphant cry of victory. At the sight, all the Immortals were struck with astonishment and filled with awe. The goddess became Zeus' favourite child, and his preference for her was so marked that it aroused the jealousy of the other gods.

JUSTICE

Athene's warlike proclivities were immediately apparent from her birth, but she was different from Ares the war-god in many ways. The arts of war which Athene cultivated were not based on love of conflict and bloodshed. Rather, they sprang from high principles and the cool recognition of the necessity of battle to uphold and preserve truth. She was a strategist rather than a brute fighter, and she balanced Ares' physical aggression and force with logic, diplomacy and cleverness. She protected the brave and valorous, and became the guardian of many heroes. But the protection she offered to Perseus, Odysseus and other famous warriors always consisted of weapons which had to be used with intelligence, foresight and planning.

Athene was a striking exception to Olympian society because of her chastity. She also rendered valuable service to mankind. She taught the art of taming horses, and fostered skills and crafts such as weaving and embroidery. Her activities were concerned not only with useful work, but with artistic creation as well. Thus she was a civilizing goddess, although a warrior when it became necessary to protect the peaceful civilization she nurtured.

On an inner level, Athene, goddess of Justice, is an image of the uniquely human faculty of reflective judgement and rational thought. To the Greeks, this faculty was divine, because it differentiated man from the beasts. Thus they envisaged Athene born from the head of great Zeus, uncontaminated by a corporeal mother who might link her with the physical and instinctual world which we share with the animals. Athene's judgements are not based on personal feeling, but upon impartial objective assessment of all the factors contained in a situation, and on ethical principles which stand as firm guidelines for choice. Athene's chastity may be taken as a symbol of the intactness and purity of this reflective faculty, which is not influenced by personal desire. Her teaching of the civilizing arts also reflects the capacity of the mind to hold untamed nature in check and transform it through clarity and objective planning. Her willingness to battle for principles rather than passions springs from the mind's capacity to make choices based upon reflection, holding the instincts in control.

JUSTICE

The card of Justice is the first of four cards in the Major Arcana which were traditionally called the Four Moral Lessons. These cards – Justice, Temperance, Strength, and the Hermit – are all concerned with the development of those individual faculties necessary for us to function effectively in life. They all contribute to what psychology calls the formation of the ego, which means the sense of 'I' that each of us must have in order to experience a sense of worth and value in life, and to cope with life's challenges from a stable and truly individual base. The Fool, having passed through the two great challenges of youth – erotic desire and aggression – now faces the necessity of building his character and developing faculties which will help him to deal with the great range of life's experiences. Thus, when the Fool meets Athene, goddess of Justice, he must learn how to think clearly and how to cultivate the faculty of a balanced mind. He must learn to weigh one thing against another – something he could not yet do in the card of the Lovers – and come to the most impartial judgement possible. Justice is not possible unless we respect fairness and truth as important ethical principles rather than as nice behaviour which we adopt because we want to be liked by others. Athene raises us above nature, and represents our striving toward a perfection conceived by the human mind and spirit.

On a divinatory level, the card of Justice appearing in a spread implies the need for balanced thought and impartial decision-making. But like Athene's sword, this card can be double-edged. There are spheres of life where Athene's cool reflection is too chilly, too idealistic, and too destructive to the warmth of personal relationship. Her sword can cut the heart with general truths which are inappropriate for a particular situation. Thus Justice is, like all the Major Arcana, an ambivalent figure. The Fool must develop what Athene represents, but he cannot stay forever in her pure temple, and must pass on to the next Moral Lesson.

TEMPERANCE

The card of Temperance portrays a beautiful black-haired young woman garbed in rainbow-coloured robes, and bearing wings of many hues. She stands with one foot in a clear stream and one foot on dry land. Along the sides of the stream-bed grow purple irises. Behind her in the sky stretches a rainbow. In her hands she holds two cups, one of gold and one of silver, and pours water from one to the other.

The rainbow, appearing as the sun shines through departing rain-clouds, symbolizes promise and the renewal of relationship. It is also a bridge between heaven and earth, again suggesting relationship.

The gold and silver cups reflect the sun and moon, masculine and feminine, conscious and unconscious, joined by the flow of feeling.

The polarity of water and earth upon which Iris stands again reflects her capacity to unite opposites within the individual.

Here we meet Iris, goddess of the rainbow and messenger to Hera, queen of the gods. Iris was the feminine counterpart of Hermes, Zeus' emissary, and was beloved by both gods and mortals because of her kind, loving nature. If Hera or Zeus wished to make their will known to men, Iris flew lightly down to earth where she either borrowed mortal shape or appeared in her divine form, that of a beautiful winged woman. Sometimes she cleaved the air as swiftly as the west wind, Zephyrus, who was her consort. At other times she glided down the rainbow which bridged sky and earth. She sped through the waters with equal ease. Even the underworld opened before her when, at the command of Zeus, she went to refill her golden cup with the waters of the Styx by which the Immortals bound themselves with fearful oaths. When the gods returned to

TEMPERANCE

Olympus from their journeys, Iris would unharness the steeds from their chariots and give the travellers nectar and ambrosia.

Iris not only delivered Hera's messages, but also effected her vengeance, although more often she offered help and care. She prepared Hera's bath, helped her with her toilet, and night and day stood at the foot of her mistress' throne. In one version of the myth it was Iris, rather than Aphrodite, who gave birth to Eros, the god of love.

On an inner level, Iris, goddess of the rainbow, is an image of the second of the qualities or faculties which the Fool must learn to form a stable individuality: a balanced heart. Where Athene, who embodies Justice, is fair and objective, Iris, who embodies Temperance, is kind and merciful, although her sympathy is neither mawkish nor sentimental. Iris is connected with the function of feeling, which is different from what we call emotion, because emotion is a visceral reaction to a situation, while feeling is an active, intelligent faculty of choice. The function of feeling is a constantly changing bridge between opposites, a careful sensing of the needs of a particular situation with the goal of harmony and relationship at the end. Thus Iris pours water ceaselessly back and forth from one cup to another, because feeling must constantly flow and renew itself according to the requirements of each moment. Where Athene's ethical precepts are necessarily static and universal, Iris' goal of harmony requires a perpetually fluid adjustment of feeling, sometimes positive and sometimes negative. Thus she can offer solicitous care or effect Hera's vengeance. But ultimately she serves the feminine realm rather than the masculine, and whatever the changing responses of the flow – even anger and conflict – the goal is always co-operation, harmony and better relationship.

We do not ordinarily think of feeling as an intelligent function like rational thought. Yet the two cards of Justice and Temperance stand as opposites and as complements. Athene and Iris are two contradictory images, one serving the Father from whose head she has sprung, the other the Mother, one upholding abstract truth even at the expense of the individual heart, the other protecting the individual heart even at the expense of abstract truth. Although these goddesses were not

TEMPERANCE

enemies in myth – for Iris was no one's enemy – yet they can be enemies within us, for they will often offer different solutions to the same problem. Do we make a decision based on rational thought, or on the dictates of what our feelings tell us is the appropriate path for the preservation of relationship? The presence of these two figures in sequence in the Major Arcana suggests that the Fool, who is really each one of us, must integrate both. Thus, having learned through Athene to think clearly, the Fool encounters Iris, goddess of the rainbow, and must learn the delicate assessment of feeling which is so different from wild reactive emotion or hypocritical sentimentality.

But even Iris, goddess of the rainbow, can be ambivalent. The constant shifting of feeling to preserve relationship can produce stagnation, because nothing but feeling makes it impossible to breathe. Nothing can be talked about, no differences discussed, no conflicts that might lead to growth, because harmony is all. Such a state allows no room for separateness, for separateness threatens aloneness, and Iris, who is friend to both gods and mortals and can function on every level of life, must yet always devotedly serve someone, and cannot exist in her own right. Thus, Temperance without Justice becomes stagnant water, where no change is allowed to occur, and the mind suffocates from sheer boredom.

On a divinatory level, the appearance of Temperance in a spread implies the need for a flow of feeling in relationship. Iris, guardian of the rainbow, suggests the potential for harmony and cooperation resulting in a good relationship or a happy marriage. We are challenged with the issue of learning to develop a balanced heart, while also being gently reminded that the Fool cannot remain forever even with the beautiful Iris, and must pass on to the next Moral Lesson.

STRENGTH

The card of Strength portrays a muscular, powerfully built man with curling chestnut hair, wearing only a red loincloth. He is engaged in a savage struggle with a lion, and has managed to wrap his strong hands around the beast's throat; at the critical moment he is winning the fight. Around man and lion loom the rocky walls of a dark cave. Through the mouth of the cave can be seen a barren landscape of brown hills.

The lion can only be conquered with bare hands; there are no man-made tools or shortcuts, but only one's own resources.

The darkness of the cave is like the darkness of the unconscious in which the primitive instincts dwell, invisible to ordinary awareness.

Heracles wears the blood-red colour of Ares, whom we met in the card of the Chariot, because he has already learned the lesson of harnessing his aggression and directing it toward a creative end.

Here we meet the great warrior Heracles, called Hercules by the Romans, who in myth was the most invincible of heroes. He was the son of Zeus, king of the gods, by a mortal woman called Alcmene. Zeus' wife Hera was, as usual, jealous of the child born from her husband's adultery, and persecuted the hero with terrible punishments. She drove him mad, and in his madness he inadvertently murdered his wife and children. Heracles begged the gods for some task to expiate his crimes, and the oracle at Delphi ordered him to subject himself to twelve years of arduous labours in the service of the evil King Eurystheus, whom Hera favoured. Thus the hero voluntarily bound himself to the servant of the goddess who persecuted him, in expiation of a crime for which she was ultimately responsible.

The first of the famous Twelve Labours which King Eurystheus

STRENGTH

required Heracles to perform was the conquest of the Nemean Lion, an enormous beast with a pelt that was proof against iron, bronze and stone. Since the lion had depopulated the neighbourhood, Heracles could find no one who could direct him to its lair. Eventually he found the beast, bespattered with blood from the day's slaughter. He shot a flight of arrows at it, but they rebounded harmlessly from the thick pelt. Next he used his sword, which bent, and then his club, which shattered on the lion's head. Heracles then netted one entrance of the two-mouthed cave in which the lion hid, and crept in by the other entrance. The lion bit off one of his fingers, but Heracles managed to catch hold of its neck and choked it to death with his bare hands. Then he flayed the pelt of the lion with its own razor-sharp claws, and forever after wore the skin as armour with the head as a helmet, thus becoming as invincible as was the beast itself.

On an inner level, Heracles battling the Nemean Lion is an image of the problem of containing the powerful and savage beast within us, while still preserving those animal qualities which are creative and vital. The lion is a special kind of beast, and reflects a different aspect of the human psyche than do the wilful horses in the card of the Chariot. The lion in myth has always been associated with royalty, even when it is at its most destructive, and this king of beasts is an image of the infantile, savage and totally egocentric beginnings of a unique individuality. Thus the Nemean Lion is not wholly evil, but possesses a magical skin which can offer invincibility. This invincibility is connected with the sense of inner permanence which comes from a solid sense of 'me'. When we wear the skin of the lion which we have conquered, the opinions of others – the great They who strike such fear into the hearts of the timid – mean little, for we are armoured in our own indestructible sense of identity.

However promising its potential, the lion is savage and vicious in its animal form. This side of a person unleashed is the 'me first' drive which will happily destroy anyone or anything in its path, so long as one's own gratification is assured. Rage is one of the manifestations of this drive – not healthy anger which might be appropriate to a situation,

STRENGTH

but a furious, explosive, floor-beating tantrum when we do not get our way. Implacable pride is another of its faces – not self-respect, but a bombast and inflated self-importance which can make us savage and unrelenting toward those upon whom we are dependent or who steal the limelight from us. The lion is in many ways like the angry infant in us, demanding that the world revolve around oneself, and destroying blindly and at random when it does not. But if this beast is conquered, then we can appropriate the magical skin, which in psychological terms means integrating the vital power of the beast and making it serve a conscious and responsible ego. Thus Heracles' conquest of the lion is not truly a killing, but a kind of transformation, so that the strength and determination of the animal are expressed by a human and not a beast. Herein lies the ambivalence of the card of Strength, for Heracles could easily simply destroy the beast without any benefit accruing from the slaughter. This is the negative face of Heracles within us: the kind of strength which represses all instinct without any transformation, leaving behind a strong shell within which lives a soul without passion, without anger, and without a true identity.

On a divinatory level, the card of Strength, when it appears in a spread, implies a situation where a collision with the lion within is inevitable, and where a creative handling of one's own rage and senseless pride is desirable. Courage, strength and self-discipline are necessary to battle with the situation. Through such an experience we can come in contact with the beast, but also with that part of us which is Heracles, the hero who can subdue it. Thus the Fool, having developed the faculties of mind and feeling, now learns to deal with his own ferocious egotism, emerging from this contest with trust in himself and integrity toward others.

THE HERMIT

The card of the Hermit portrays an old man with a grey beard, shrouded in grey robes with his face half-hidden by a cowl. In his right hand he carries a lamp which burns with a bright golden light. In his left hand he wields a scythe. A crow perches on his shoulder. Behind him a cold, misty landscape of grey mountains bleeds into an oppressive grey sky.

The lamp which Cronos carries is the lamp of insight and understanding, gleaned from the loneliness and patient waiting which the card of the Hermit implies.

The crow is Cronos' bird because it was believed to be the embodiment of the spirit of the old king who has died to make way for the new cycle.

The crescent blade of the scythe is also the crescent of the moon, given to Cronos by his mother Gaea, and symbolizing the eternal fluctuations and cycles of time.

Here we meet the ancient god Cronos, whose name means Time. In myth, Uranus (Heaven) and Gaea (Earth) mated and produced the first race, the Titans or earth-gods, of whom Cronos was the youngest. But Uranus regarded his progeny with horror, for they were ugly and imperfect and made of flesh. Thus he shut the Titans up in the depths of the underworld so that they might not offend his eyes. But Gaea grew angry and meditated a terrible vengeance upon her husband. From her bosom she drew forth flint, fashioned a sharp scythe, and gave it to the astute Cronos, her last-born. When evening fell Uranus came as usual to rejoin his wife. While he unsuspectingly slept, Cronos, who with his mother's aid lay in hiding, armed himself with the scythe, castrated his father, and cast the bleeding genitals into the sea.

THE HERMIT

Cronos then liberated his brothers and became sovereign of the earth. Under his long, patient reign the work of Creation was completed. This time on earth became known as the Golden Age, because of the abundance over which Cronos presided. As god of time he ruled over the orderly passage of the seasons, birth and growth followed by death and gestation and rebirth, and was worshipped both as a grim reaper who set the boundaries past which man and nature could not go, and as a god of fertility. But Cronos could not himself accept the cyclical laws which he had inaugurated, for when it was prophesied that one day his own son would overthrow him as he had his father Uranus, he swallowed his children as they were born so that he could preserve his rule unchanged. Thus follows the story of Zeus, the youngest of Cronos' children, whom we met in the card of the Emperor and who in myth overthrew Cronos and ushered in the reign of the Olympian gods. Cronos was banished, some say to the depths of the underworld, but others say to the Blessed Isles where he sleeps, awaiting the beginning of a new Golden Age.

On an inner level Cronos, the Hermit, is an image of the last of the four Moral Lessons which the Fool must learn: the lesson of time and the limitations of mortal life. Nothing is allowed to live beyond its span, and nothing remains unchanged; and this is a simple and obvious facet of life which despite its simplicity and obviousness is painful for us to learn and often only comes with age and hard experience. Cronos is a god who both embodies the meaning of time and also rebels against it. So he is humbled and overthrown, and learns wisdom in solitude and silence. In many ways he is an image of the body itself, which inexorably grows older yet rebels against its mortal fate. The problem of solitude and the discovery that one is ultimately alone and mortal are dilemmas which all human beings must face. Acceptance of this condition is also, in a mysterious way, a true inner separation from the parents and from childhood, because it means the sacrifice of the fantasy that someday, somewhere, someone will come and magically make it all better. 'And then they lived happily ever after' is a sentiment that cannot survive in Cronos' world. Youth passes into maturity, and

THE HERMIT

can never be regained in any concrete way; but memory and wisdom are distilled from the passage of time, and also the gift of patience.

The lesson of the Hermit is one which cannot be learned through struggle and conquest. Thus Cronos stands in counterpoint to Heracles, for struggle will not stop time. Only acceptance of time yields the rewards of Cronos' Golden Age. Through enforced limitation and through circumstances which only time, not battle, can release, the Fool develops the reflective, introverted, solitary stance of Cronos the Hermit. Thus Cronos is in some ways an image of humility, which often begins with humiliation in the face of that which we cannot change, but which can result in a quality of stillness and serenity without which we cannot endure the obstacles and disappointments which life sometimes brings. However clever the intellect, however warm the heart, however strong the sense of identity, the vicissitudes of life would shatter us if we were unable to find somewhere within the patience and prudence of the Hermit, who teaches us how to endure and wait in silence. The negative face of Cronos is calcification, a stubborn resistance to change and the passage of time. But the creative face of this ancient and ambivalent god is the shrewdness to change what we can, to accept what we cannot, and to wait in silence until we can tell the difference.

On a divinatory level, the card of Cronos, the Hermit, augurs a time of aloneness or withdrawal from the extraverted activities of life, so that the wisdom of patience may be acquired. There is an opportunity to build solid foundations if one is willing to wait. Thus the Fool at last arrives at maturity, having developed a mind and a heart, a firm sense of identity and finally a deep respect for his own limitations in the great passage of the round of time.

THE WHEEL OF FORTUNE

The card of the Wheel of Fortune portrays three women seated within a dark cave. The first is young, and spins thread from a golden spindle. The second is handsome and mature, and measures a length of the thread between her hands. The third is old, and holds a pair of shears. In the centre between them is a golden wheel, around which four small human figures can be seen in different positions. Through the mouth of the cave a rich green landscape is visible.

The cave suggests both the womb from which life springs and the tomb to which it returns – the beginning and end of fate.

The three ages of the Moirai reflect the lunar phases – young crescent, full, and finally dark, the three stages of every human life.

THE WHEEL OF FORTUNE

The thread which the Moirai spin, measure and cut is likened to the weaving of the tissues of the body which takes place in the womb, thus suggesting that fate is bound up with heredity and with the body itself.

Here we meet the three goddesses of Fate, whom the Greeks called the Moirai. In myth, the Moirai were the daughters of Mother Night, conceived without a father. Clotho was the spinner, Lachesis the measurer, and Atropos, whose name means 'she who cannot be avoided', the cutter. The three Fates wove the thread of a human life in the secret darkness of their cave, and their work could not be undone by any god, not even great Zeus. Once the destiny of an individual was woven, it was irrevocable, and could not be altered; and the length of life and the time of death were part and parcel of the share which the Moirai allotted. If an individual tried to challenge fate, as the heroes sometimes did, then they were afflicted with what was called *hubris*, which means arrogance in the face of the gods. Such an

THE WHEEL OF FORTUNE

individual could not of course evade his or her fate, and was sometimes punished terribly by the gods for trying to overstep the boundaries set by the Moirai. In one myth, it was said that Apollo the sun-god once laughed at the Moirai and mischievously made them drunk in order to save his friend Admetus from death. But usually it was believed that Zeus himself walked in awe of the Fates, because they were not the children of any god, but rather the progeny of the depths of the Night, which was the oldest power in the universe.

On an inner level, the three Moirai who hold the Wheel of Fortune present an image of a deep and mysterious law at work within the individual, which is unknown and unseen yet which seems to precipitate sudden changes of fortune that overturn the established pattern of life. The four human figures on the Wheel represent different experiences of fortune, for when life intrudes in this way we do not at first look behind the Wheel to the source, but are preoccupied with our reactions to the change. The man at the top has been catapulted into success through the turning of the Wheel, while the man at the bottom has been broken by what he believes to be 'bad luck' – not luck at all, but rather the visible signature of some mysterious pattern at work. The man on the right has begun his climb, helped by that same unseen power which has crowned one person and broken another; while the man on the left, against his will, has begun his descent, for the Wheel has turned and his 'luck' is running out.

But the card of the Wheel of Fortune is not really about sudden turns of luck, chance or accident. Behind the Wheel stand the Moirai, and there is an intelligent and orderly plan behind the apparently random changes in life. These ancient figures are within us, deep in the womb of the unconscious, although they are not part of the conscious personality. We only become aware of them through their outward effects, which feel like Fate, yet which spring not from some external power but from within the depths of the soul.

The experience of the Wheel of Fortune is really an experience of that 'Other' within us, which ordinarily we project onto the world outside, thus blaming sudden changes of fortune on someone or something

THE WHEEL OF FORTUNE

besides ourselves. The turn of the Wheel of Fortune forces us to become aware of this Other, the intelligent movement behind the Wheel which is the destiny we each carry within us. The image of the Wheel itself is a profound one, for the moving rim of the Wheel is like the moving panorama of life which we encounter; but the hub remains still at the centre, a constant and unchanging essence or source. The hub is thus like the hidden Self which 'chooses' (although it is no choice of the conscious ego) to turn itself toward various situations, events, paths and people. Fate does not come to meet us; rather, we turn to meet our fate. In the card of the High Priestess, the Fool meets that intuitive faculty within himself, personified by Persephone, which can glimpse this pattern at work. Here, in the card of the Wheel of Fortune, the Fool encounters that which weaves the design, the source of life itself, aloof and invisible, older than the oldest of gods, with an absolute power that even the king of the gods dares not challenge. Even the spirit is subject to the commands of this invisible centre which the Greeks imaged as the three Fates, and which shakes us from our complacency and our illusion of control.

The unease and even fear which some people have of studies such as the Tarot, astrology and other mantic arts perhaps spring in part from the anxiety which arises when the conscious personality, used to decision-making and the fantasy of omnipotent will, confronts this Other in the depths. Although it too belongs to us, it is not within our power to control, just as Zeus must walk in awe of the Moirai. Thus the Wheel of Fortune is more than a significator of change. It is a herald of a profound inner journey through which the Fool, the image of ourselves, gradually comes to terms with his own destiny.

On a divinatory level, the Wheel of Fortune augurs a sudden change of fortune. This may be 'good' or 'bad', but whichever way the Wheel turns it brings growth and a new phase of life. We cannot predict what will come to meet us – or rather, what we will turn to meet. But behind these changes stand the Moirai, an image of the centre within. Thus the Fool is thrown from his complacency, and begins the descent to his own source.

THE HANGED MAN

The card of the Hanged Man portrays a mature man with brown hair and beard. Although he is shackled in a tortuous position, nearly naked, to the bare face of a cliff, still he wears a serene expression on his face. Behind him looms a dark landscape of craggy rocks, while a setting sun casts a bloody glow across his body and illumines his head. Above him, an eagle approaches.

The setting sun suggests the waning of the bright light of consciousness and will.

Prometheus' posture implies that the head – the rational mind – no longer controls. Like the setting sun, this image symbolizes the descent of the spirit into the darkness of the unconscious.

The liver, which in the myth was attacked by Zeus' eagle, was associated with spirit and hope. Thus Prometheus' torment is an image of the loss of faith, which in mystical teaching is called the 'dark night of the soul', where one can only wait without a confident vision of how it will all end.

Here we meet Prometheus, the Titan who defied the law of Zeus and stole the fire of the gods to give to man, knowing full well that he would suffer for his deed. The name Prometheus means 'foresight', and the Titan possessed the gift of prophecy. He was also said in myth to have created man out of earth and the water of his own tears, while Athene breathed life into the creation. Thus Prometheus had a deep sympathy for the lot of humankind, for he had made them.

But Zeus asserted his divine supremacy over men by withholding fire from them. This meant that there could be no progress or illumination, for without fire man was condemned to live like the beasts, eating raw meat and hiding in caves. Prometheus took some of the holy fire from Hephaistos' forge, hid it in a hollow fennel stalk, and carried it to earth.

THE HANGED MAN

Outraged by the theft, Zeus resolved to annihilate mankind by flood to destroy the offenders, for not only was his pride injured, but with fire man might attempt to become godlike. But Prometheus warned his son Deucalion, who built an ark and went on board with his wife, Pyrrha. The flood lasted for nine days and nights, but on the tenth day the deluge ceased and Deucalion offered up sacrifice to Zeus. The king of the gods, touched by his piety, agreed to his request to renew the human race.

But Prometheus did not get off so lightly. As he had foreseen, Zeus seized and bound him with indestructible chains to a high cliff in the Caucasus mountains. An eagle flew down each day to devour Prometheus' liver; each night the liver was renewed and the torture continued. After thirty years, Zeus permitted his rescue by the hero Heracles, who slew the eagle and broke the prisoner's chains. Prometheus was made immortal, while grateful mankind, honouring their benefactor, raised altars to him and for the first time wore rings, in commemoration of his bondage.

On an inner level, Prometheus, the Hanged Man, is an image of voluntary sacrifice for a greater good. This sacrifice can be of an external thing or an inner attitude, but it is made with willingness and a full acceptance of the suffering that might be required. In the card of the Wheel of Fortune, the Fool encountered those sudden blows of fate which inaugurate far-reaching changes in life. But we, like the Fool, can respond to such changes in many ways. Some people cannot adapt, and cling to the past which they have lost. Others become bitter and blame life, or God, or society, or another person. The image of Prometheus is a symbol of that part of us which has the foresight necessary to understand that such changes might be needed for the unfoldment of an inner design which is not yet clear. Thus, the Titan represents an attitude of willing submission to that mysterious centre whose workings lie behind the turnings of the Wheel.

Prometheus, the Hanged Man, implies an acceptance of waiting in darkness. He is in suspension, tortured by anxiety and the fear that his sacrifice might in the end come to nothing; yet he wears a peaceful

THE HANGED MAN

expression. And his suspension ends at last, altering both him and his relationship with the gods, for he is given immortality. In many ways, Prometheus is an image of the relinquishing of control so that a new and greater sense of life can emerge. Because Prometheus has made man, it could be said that he is man – a kind of visionary spirit within us which sees greater possibilities and is willing to abandon all that we have previously held sacred so that this greater consciousness might be obtained. As a result, Prometheus is at first made terribly vulnerable, for if we are prepared to make such a sacrifice on trust then we open ourselves to life, and life can hurt us. But this price of giving up our defenses and making the journey into loneliness and self-doubt seems to be necessary for any real sense of what supports us when we cannot support ourselves. It is what religions mean by true faith, and it can only be gained through risking ourselves in life. The card of the Hanged Man is a natural outgrowth of the turning of the Wheel of Fortune, for it implies a willingness to trust in that Other which knows better than the ego what might be right and necessary for one's development.

On a divinatory level, Prometheus, the Hanged Man, augurs the need for a voluntary sacrifice for the purpose of acquiring something of greater value. This might be the sacrifice of an external thing which has previously provided security, in the hope that some potential can be given room to develop. Or it can be the sacrifice of a cherished attitude, such as intellectual superiority, or unforgiving hatred, or a stubborn pursuit of some unobtainable fantasy. Thus the Fool responds to the challenge of the turning of the Wheel with a willingness to put his trust in the unseen workings of the unconscious, and waits – often with fear and anxiety – in the hope of a new and better life.

DEATH

The card of Death portrays a figure shrouded in black robes, his face hidden beneath a dark helmet. His hands are open to receive the gifts offered by the tiny human figures who kneel before him. One gives him a golden crown, another a pile of coins. The third, a child, hands him a flower. Behind this dark figure a leaden river flows. On the near side of the river the earth is cracked and barren. On the far shore, the land slowly brightens and turns green beneath a rising sun.

The River Styx, which means 'hated', was envisaged as a leaden and forbidding river, because it represents a stage we must pass through in order to reach the riches of the underworld. This is the state of sadness and mourning, which are as necessary to life as joy and celebration.

The rising sun suggests a new future, although the souls who kneel before Hades are still unaware of it.

The child who offers the flower is an image of the childlike trust in change which can help us to deal with the process of mourning. Only the child is unafraid of expressing grief.

Here we meet the dark god Hades, lord of the underworld, whom we first encountered in the card of the Empress as the abductor of Demeter's daughter Persephone. In myth, Hades was known as the Invisible. He was also called Pluto, which means 'riches', because his realm was full of hidden wealth. Hades was a son of the Titans Cronos and Rhea, who was rescued by his brother Zeus when Cronos had disgorged his children. Zeus then gave Hades the kingdom of the underworld as his share of the inheritance. Over this domain the dark god ruled as absolute master. When he emerged into the daylight world, his helmet rendered him invisible, so that no mortal could see him. The rites of death required that a gold coin be placed in the mouth of the corpse, for without offering Hades his due the soul would be doomed to wander forever on the shores of the River Styx which bounded the underworld kingdom.

Although Hades was accorded less status than his heavenly brother Zeus, he possessed the greater power, because his law was irrevocable. Once a soul entered the kingdom of Hades, no god, not even the king of the gods, could retrieve it again. Although certain heroes such as Orpheus and Theseus made illicit entry into Hades' realm, tricking the ancient boatman Charon and managing to avoid the terrible three-headed dog Cerberus who guarded the gates, none of them returned to the upper world the same. Such was the irrevocable power of Hades that the gods swore their oaths by the waters of his river Styx, which was both deadly poison and also conferred immortality.

On an inner level, Hades, lord of Death, is an image of the permanent and final end of a cycle of life. When we change, a new attitude or new circumstances may come, but the old way is dead and will never return in its original form. Thus Hades is a symbol of that finality which we experience with all endings, and also, portrayed by the dark robes, a symbol of the experience of mourning which is necessary to prepare for the new cycle. In the card of the Hanged Man, we encountered the experience of voluntary submission to the hidden laws of the psyche – the decision to let go of something in the hope that a new phase of life might emerge. Hades, the lord of Death, represents that in-between state where we are brought face to face with the complete irrevocability of our loss, before the sense of new growth has begun.

The card of Death does not necessarily symbolize a 'bad' ending. The experience of irrevocable ending can accompany such joyful events as marriage or the birth of a child. But these events not only connote a new beginning; they also mean the death of an old way of life, and that loss must be acknowledged and mourned. Thus we have such modern rituals as 'stag parties' to acknowledge the loss of the bachelor state. Women (and men, for that matter) are often unaccountably depressed at the birth of a child, because there has not yet been an acknowledgement that a phase of life has died at the same time that a new thing has been born. Thus, coin must be paid to Hades, because he presides over

DEATH

all endings and new beginnings, and the ending is as important as the beginning and must be recognized and felt. We go naked into the underworld, for we cannot bring with us our previous patterns and attitudes which have provided us with security. Thus the card of Death is not a description of physical death, but rather an image of the inevitable changing cycles of life which always contain endings. Through the eyes of Hades, life can be seen as a constant procession of deaths, beginning with the leaving of the comforting waters of the womb for the harsh reality of separate physical existence. Never again will we live in the blissful paradise of the mother's body. Childhood must die for adolescence and sexual development to begin, and youth, however strenuously we prolong it with diet, exercise and cosmetics, will eventually die to make way for the maturity of middle age. Every relationship, even the best, has its cycles of endings and beginnings, for our feelings change as time passes and our understanding of another person grows. We leave our single state behind in marriage, and our eternal youth behind with the birth of children who remind us of our own mortality. Thus Hades, the lord of Death, is our invisible companion throughout life, to whom we must pay our due.

On a divinatory level, the card of Death implies that something must come to an end. Whether or not this experience is painful depends upon the person's capacity to accept and recognize the necessity of endings. The card of Death can augur an opportunity for a new life, if one can let go of the old one. Thus the Fool enters the underworld, leaving behind him his previous life, to prepare for an unknown future.

THE DEVIL

The card of the Devil portrays a Satyr, a creature which is half man and half goat, dancing to the music of the pipes which he holds in his left hand. In his right, he grasps two lengths of chain, each attached to a collar around the neck of a naked human figure. The figures – a man and a woman – wear tiny horns like those of the Satyr. Although their hands and feet are free to dance, they are held by their chains of fear and fascination for the music. Around them loom the dark walls of a cave.

The goat in myth was associated with lechery and dirtiness, and was considered an unclean and lustful animal. But the goat also symbolizes the scapegoat, the person or thing upon whom people project the inferior side of themselves in order to feel cleaner and more righteous. Thus Pan, the Devil, is the scapegoat within which we blame for our troubles in life.

THE DEVIL

The dark and doorless cave implies that Pan dwells in the most inaccessioous realm of the unconscioous. Only crisis can break through the wall into his secret chamber.

The dancing figures are free, if they so wish, to remove their chains, for their hands are not bound. Bondage to the Devil is ultimately a voluntary matter which consciousness can release.

Here we meet the great god Pan, whom the Greeks worshipped as the Great All. In myth, Hermes fathered Pan on the nymph Dryope. The child was so ugly at birth – with horns, beard, tail and goat-legs – that his mother ran away from him in fright, and Hermes carried him up to Olympus for the gods' amusement. Pan haunted the woods and pastures of Arcadia, and personified the fertile, phallic spirit of wild, untamed nature. But he could also occasionally be friendly to men, guarding flocks, herds, and beehives. He took part in the revels of the mountain-nymphs and helped hunters to find their quarry. On one occasion he pursued the chaste nymph Syrinx to the River Ladon, where she transformed herself into a water-reed to escape his unwelcome hairy embraces. There, since

THE DEVIL

he could not distinguish her from all the rest, he cut several reeds at random, and made them into a syrinx or Pan-pipe.

From Pan's name we derive the word 'panic', because he amused himself by giving the lonely traveller sudden frights. He was despised by the other gods, but they exploited his powers. Apollo the sun-god wheedled the art of prophecy from him, and Hermes copied a pipe which he had let fall, claimed it as his own invention, and sold it to Apollo. Thus the brilliant sun-god received both his music and his prophecy illicitly from the goatish, ugly and untamed god of nature.

On an inner level, Pan, the Devil, is an image of bondage to the crudest, most instinctual aspect of human nature. Because the god was worshipped in caves and grottoes, attended by fear, his image within us suggests something that we both fear and are fascinated by – the raw, goatish, uncivilized sexual impulses which we experience as evil because of their compulsive nature. Since the dawn of the Christian era, the god Pan has been appropriated into the figure of the Devil, complete with goat-horns and leering grin, and he is despised by 'spiritual' folk as Apollo once despised him in Greek myth. Plutarch recounts how, during the reign of the Emperor Tiberius, a mariner sailing near the Echinades Islands heard a mysterious voice call out to him three times, saying: 'When you reach Palodes, proclaim that the great god Pan is dead.' This was at the same moment that Christianity was born in Judaea. But the presence of this card among the Major Arcana of the Tarot suggests that Pan did not die. Rather, he has been relegated to the nethermost recesses of the unconscious, representing that which we fear, loathe and despise in ourselves, yet which holds us in bondage through our very fear and disgust.

The problem of shame about the body and the sexual impulses, particularly those impulses which psychoanalysis has done so much to bring into the light in this century – incest fantasies, fascination with bodily functions and excretions, the feeling of being dirty and wicked, goatish and hairy, ugly and inferior – is the problem which Pan, the Devil, personifies. Even the most sexually 'liberated' man or woman can experience this secret shame about the body. We may find something

THE DEVIL

noble and romantic about the raging lion in the card of Strength, or the wilful horses of the Chariot. But it is more difficult to perceive nobility in Pan. Yet in myth he was not evil, merely untamed, amoral and natural. It is the paralysis of the humans who are held enthralled in terror and fascination which creates the problem. The card of the Devil implies blocks and inhibitions, usually sexual, which arise from our lack of understanding of Pan. Although he is ugly, he is the Great All – the raw life of the body itself, amoral and crude, but nonetheless a god. The energy which is expended in keeping the Devil in his cave, shameful and hidden, is energy which is lost to the personality, but which can be released with immensely powerful effect if one is willing to look Pan in the face. Thus the Fool must learn to confront with humility the basest and most shameful aspects of himself, or he will remain forever in bondage to his own fear. Then, in order to hide this shameful secret, he must pretend that he is superior and projects his own bestiality on others, leading to prejudice, bigotry and even persecution of individuals and races who seem to him 'evil'.

On a divinatory level, the card of Pan, the Devil, implies the necessity of a confrontation with all that is shadowy, shameful and base in the personality. The Fool must free himself by gaining knowledge and honest, humble acceptance of Pan, for then he can release the creative power which is held in chains by his own panic and self-disgust. Thus he comes to the heart of the labyrinth and faces his own darkness in the essential darkness of his body, in order to become what he always was – merely natural.

THE TOWER

The card of the Tower portrays a stone edifice built on a high rock overlooking the sea. From the depths of the water a powerful, menacing figure emerges, crowned with gold, brown hair streaming with seaweed, with a fish's tail that can be seen between the angry waves. He points his trident at the building, which is struck by a flash of lightning and cracks open. The sea boils and the sky is black and ominous, lit by stormy red flashes.

The trident is Poseidon's attribute of power, reflecting the lunar crescent which links him with the realm of the instincts and the night.

The god's eruption from the sea suggests a powerful instinctual force emerging from the unconscious, stronger than the will's efforts to repress it.

Although Poseidon is an earth-god, he is portrayed with a fish's tail. This links him with the cold-blooded sea creatures, far away from warm-blooded human life, which belong to the archaic world of the instincts.

Here we see the famous Labyrinth of King Minos, which was struck by an earthquake when the angry god Poseidon rose up from the waters to topple the kingdom. In myth, Minos was the wealthy and powerful king of Crete. He was given this power by Poseidon, god of earthquakes and the ocean depths, who agreed to make Minos sovereign of the seas if the king offered a beautiful white bull in sacrifice to the god. But King Minos did not want to give up the bull, and hid it in his herd, substituting a lesser animal in its place. In fury at this act of arrogance and repudiation of the pact, Poseidon called upon the love-goddess Aphrodite for aid. She afflicted Minos' wife Pasiphae with a consuming passion for the white bull. The queen bribed the palace artisan Daedalus to build her a wooden cow. Pasiphae entered the cow, the bull entered Pasiphae, and from this

THE TOWER

union of queen and beast was born the Minotaur, the shame of Minos, a horrible creature with a man's body and a bull's head which fed on human flesh. In terror the king hid this creature at the heart of a great stone Labyrinth which he ordered Daedalus to build.

But the kingdom could not remain forever in such a stagnant state, with such a shameful secret hidden at its core. With the help of Minos' daughter Ariadne, the hero Theseus, son of Poseidon, came and slew the Minotaur, and the god at the same moment rose up in anger from his bed beneath the sea and struck at the Labyrinth. The building was reduced to rubble by the earthquake, burying both King Minos and the corpse of the Minotaur beneath it, while all the slaves who had been held in bondage by Minos' power were set free. Theseus was proclaimed king of Crete, a new era was inaugurated, and the Labyrinth was never raised again.

On an inner level, the god-struck Tower is an image of the collapse of old forms. The Tower is the only man-made structure in the Major Arcana, and is thus a representation of structures, inner and outer, which we ourselves build, like Minos, as defenses against life and as concealment to hide our less agreeable sides from others. In many ways the Tower is an image of the socially acceptable façades we adapt to hide the beast within. Then we use our professions, our good credentials, our affiliations with respectable institutions and companies, our carefully mannered social roles, our politest smiles and most diplomatic exchanges, our magazine-inspired appearances and family-instilled morals, to hide that shameful secret which in the card of the Devil awaits the Fool in the underworld. The Tower is a structure of false or outgrown values, those attitudes toward life which do not spring from the whole self but are 'put on' like costumes in a play to impress the audience. Likewise the Tower also represents the structures we build in the outside world to embody our incomplete selves.

Thus, when the Fool confronts the great god Pan at the heart of the Labyrinth within, he is changed by the encounter. He is more humble, more complete, and more real. Inevitably, this change will result in changes occurring in outer life. Just as our attitudes are altered by any

THE TOWER

encounter with what lies in the unconscious, so too are our chosen lifestyles. One of the reasons why many people fear this inward-looking process is that they are dimly aware that, having discovered one's real nature, one can no longer pretend in the eyes of the world. Honest encounter with the Devil invokes a profound inner integrity, and thus the Tower, the edifice which represents the values of the past, must fall. The Fool perceives the ways in which he has betrayed his essential self, and this shock is like the trident of Poseidon striking the Labyrinth: It cracks open the defenses and releases those parts of ourselves which have been enslaved. In many ways the Minotaur is like the Devil, for both represent a bestial secret connected with the body and with shameful sexual feelings which must be concealed even from ourselves if we are to appear blameless and 'nice' in the eyes of society.

On a divinatory level, the card of the Tower appearing in a spread augurs the breaking down of existing forms. This card, like the cards of Death and the Devil, depends a great deal upon the attitude of the individual in terms of how difficult or painful it is to deal with. Obviously it is more creative to ask oneself where one is constricted or bound by a false persona or image, because a willing effort to break through this pretense can spare a great deal of anguish. But it seems that the Tower will fall anyway, whether we are willing or unwilling, not because some malicious external fate decrees it, but because something within the individual has reached boiling point and can no longer live within such confines.

THE STAR

The card of the Star portrays a beautiful young woman with long, fair hair, kneeling before an open chest. From the chest a noxious swarm of flying creatures rises, filling the air with darkness. But the young woman's eyes are fixed on a bright star which hovers above her, within which can be seen a female figure in glowing white robes.

Pandora is, like Eve, a woman. It is the feminine side of human nature – feeling, instinct, imagination, intuition – which must probe for the truth despite the consequences.

The insects, unlike warmer-blooded creatures, are far from human consciousness and relationship. We cannot communicate with them, but are stung and goaded by nature itself.

The chest which Zeus sends to mankind with Pandora is like the apple in the Garden of Eden: something which is forbidden yet impossible to resist. It contains knowledge of the reality of human life, which means the death of naiveté and childlike fantasy; yet it also contains the most precious attribute of the human spirit.

Here we meet Pandora, who in myth opened the chest which Zeus had maliciously given to mankind, and released all the Spites. After the Titan Prometheus had stolen the sacred fire of the gods to give to mankind, the king of the gods resolved to inflict severe punishments on the human race, which culminated in the great flood described in the card of the Hanged Man. Before this flood, however, his anger was more subtle, although not yet satisfied. Zeus ordered Hephaistos the smith-god to fashion clay and water into a body, to give it vital force and human voice, and to make a virgin whose dazzling beauty would equal that of the immortal goddesses. All the divinities heaped their special gifts on this new creature, who received the name of Pandora. Hermes, however, put perfidy into Pandora's heart and lies into her mouth. This woman Zeus sent to Epimetheus, brother of Prometheus, along with a great chest. But Epimetheus,

THE STAR

having been warned by his brother to accept no gifts from Zeus, respectfully excused himself. However, having seen the terrible vengeance which the king of the gods then inflicted upon Prometheus, Epimetheus (whose name means 'hindsight') hastened to marry Pandora.

Prometheus, before he was seized and imprisoned on his lonely mountain peak, managed to warn Epimetheus not to touch the chest, and Epimetheus conveyed this warning to Pandora with frightening threats. But Hephaistos had made Pandora as foolish, mischievous and idle as she was beautiful. Presently she opened the lid of the chest, and the terrible afflictions which Zeus had gathered – Old Age, Labour, Sickness, Insanity, Vice and Passion – escaped and spread over the earth, infecting the whole of mankind. Hope alone, which had somehow got locked in the chest with the Spites, did not fly away.

On an inner level, the image of Pandora and the Star of Hope is a symbol of that part of us which, despite disappointment, depression and loss can still cling to a sense of meaning and a future which might grow out of the unhappiness of the past. The Star does not represent a fully formed conviction of future plans, or a solution to one's problems, or a guide to action. Like the cards of the Hermit and the Hanged Man, the card of the Star is a card of waiting, for the sense of hope is a fragile light which glimmers and guides but does not dispel the darkness altogether. Hope is therefore shown as a female figure, because it is the irrational side of us – the intuition – which perceives the Star in the middle of the noxious swarm of Spites. Hope does not make the Spites go away, or undo the vengeance which Zeus has unleashed. But somehow, in some mysterious way, it offers faith, and therefore in the image Pandora's eyes are fixed not on the unhappiness of the human condition, but on this vague, irrational, inexplicable sense that soon there will be a dawn.

This quality of hope has nothing to do with planned expectations. It is connected with something deep within us which has sometimes been called the will to live, and which – despite being a subjective experience with no visible concrete reason – can often make the

THE STAR

difference between life and death. Physicians know this about an ill patient – that the individual who has a sense of hope and a will to live can often find the inner resources to battle with a disease which would otherwise kill. Likewise individuals who have suffered tragic circumstances or been faced with challenges which are far greater than the ordinary human capacity to cope – such as those who experienced the imprisonment of concentration camps in Germany and Poland during the Second World War, or saw families destroyed in the Russian invasions of Czechoslovakia in 1948 and Hungary in 1956 – have often expressed their belief that it was some inner feeling of faith and meaning that meant the difference between survival and complete collapse and death. Hope is a profound and mysterious thing, for it would seem that it can transcend anything life offers us in the way of catastrophe. Yet it does not arise from an act of will, any more than the Star of Hope appears in the myth of Pandora through any deliberate action on her part. It is simply there, mysteriously locked in the chest along with all the woes, and if the individual can perceive its delicate glimmering then one's response to difficulties is radically altered. Thus the Star, the guiding vision of hope and promise, arises not from intention but out of the ashes of the Tower which has been destroyed. The Fool waits amidst the rubble, without any clear sense of how or what to rebuild. In the midst of this confusion and collapse of old attitudes and structures, the faint, elusive yet potent Star of Hope rises.

On a divinatory level, the card of the Star when it appears in a spread portends the experience of hope, meaning and faith in the midst of difficulties. Although the Star too can be ambivalent, and can warn against blind hope without the necessary action to build upon it, the card of the Star is an augury of promise, an altogether welcome experience for the Fool who has passed through the collapse of everything which he believed to be of value in his life.

THE MOON

The card of the Moon portrays a mysterious feminine figure with three faces, crowned by a diadem of the moon in its three phases. Her hair is silvery, and she is clothed in white robes which flow into a pool at her feet. Beside her stands a three-headed dog, while from the depths of the pool a crab attempts to crawl from the water. The sky behind her is dark, lit only by the luminescence of her crown.

The three faces of Hecate, like the three faces of the Moirai, reflect the inevitable changing faces of life.

White and silver, the colours of Hecate's robes and hair, are associated with the moon because they were believed to contain all colours within them in a nascent state.

The crab is a creature which belongs wholly to neither the watery nor the earthy realm, but makes its abode in between. Thus the crab is an image of the dream-world, which arises from the unknown depths but intrudes upon the day-world in the form of powerful images and feelings which cannot be ignored.

Here we meet the ancient underworld goddess Hecate, ruler of the moon, magic and enchantment. In myth Hecate was sometimes interchangeable with Artemis the moon-goddess, although a much older deity, and was powerful both in the sky and beneath the earth. The child of Zeus and Hera, she incurred her mother's wrath by stealing a pot of rouge. She fled to earth and hid in the house of a woman who had just been brought to bed with a child. Contact with childbirth rendered her impure, and she was thus taken to the underworld to be washed of her stain. Instead she became one of the underworld rulers, and was called the Invincible Queen, presiding over purifications and expiations. As a goddess of enchantment, she sent demons to earth who tormented men through their dreams. She was accompanied by Cerberus, the three-headed guardian of the

THE MOON

underworld's gate, who was her animal form and familiar spirit. The places she most frequently haunted were crossroads, tombs and the scenes of crimes, and three-headed images sacred to her were erected at crossroads and worshipped on the eve of the full moon.

Zeus himself honoured Hecate so greatly that he never denied her the ancient power which she had always enjoyed: that of bestowing or withholding from mortals any desired gift. Her companions in the underworld were the three Erinyes or Furies, who punished offenses against nature and represented in a more threatening form the three Moirai or Fates. Thus Hecate is one of the most archaic images in myth, presiding over magic, childbirth, death, the underworld and fate.

On an inner level, Hecate, the moon-goddess, is an image of the mysterious watery depths of the unconscious. We have already encountered this strange and elusive realm in two other cards in the Major Arcana: the High Priestess and the Wheel of Fortune. These three cards are linked in meaning and represent a progression in deepening understanding and experience of the world of the unconscious. Through Persephone, the High Priestess, the Fool became aware of an intuition of his own personal depths, a secret self which lay beneath ordinary mundane life. Through the Moirai who preside over the Wheel of Fortune, he experienced the power which we call Fate, through sudden changes of fortune that reveal an invisible law or purposeful pattern within. Here, in the card of the Moon, we find in the image of Hecate an experience of the great collective sea of the unconscious from which not only the individual but the whole of life has emerged. Hecate is more than a portrayal of personal depths. She embodies the feminine principle in life itself, and the three faces and three lunar phases reflect her multifaceted power over heaven, earth and underworld. In psychological terms, it is from this oceanic realm of the human imagination that the great myths and religious symbols and works of art are born over the centuries. It is a chaotic, confusing, unbounded world of which the individual with his personal journey and search for self are only a tiny part.

The meeting with Hecate, the moon-goddess, is a confrontation with

THE MOON

a transpersonal world, where individual boundaries dissolve and the sense of direction and ego are lost. It is as though we must wait submerged in the waters of this world while the new potentials arise which will eventually become our future. But the dark waters of the collective unconscious contain both negative and positive, and it is sometimes hard to distinguish its shifting movements from madness and delusion. It can be a frightening, anxiety-provoking world, for living in the realm over which Hecate presides means living without knowledge and clarity. Something has washed over us which cleanses the past and prepares the way for the future, but we must wait as the foetus waits in the womb. The only road to Hecate's world is the 'royal road' of dreams, which like the crab tantalizes us with a glimpse and then slips back into the water again. The card of the Moon is a card of gestation, full of confusion, anxiety and bewilderment. We have nothing but the dream-world and the Star of Hope to guide us, for this image of the feminine is not a personal one like that of the High Priestess. It is vague and elusive and impersonal, embodying itself as shifting moods and confusion. Hecate is never really graspable, for she is a goddess of magic, and initiates the Fool into a world greater than himself, that primal water out of which all life comes.

On a divinatory level, the card of Hecate, the moon-goddess, augurs a period of confusion, fluctuation and uncertainty. We are in the grip of the unconscious and can do nothing but wait and cling to the elusive images of dreams and the vague sense of hope and faith. Thus the Fool awaits his rebirth in the waters of a greater womb, dimly aware that his journey of personal development is only a small fragment of a vast, unknowable life which spans millennia and which remains eternally fertile yet eternally unformed.

THE SUN

The card of the Sun portrays a classically handsome, beautifully proportioned man with golden hair, crowned with laurel leaves and bearing on his head the golden disc of the sun. He has golden wings and wears a short robe of dazzling white. In his right hand he holds a bow and a quiver of arrows; in his left he cradles a lyre. Framing him are two columns and a portico built of pale golden stone. Behind him a golden-green landscape, dotted with laurel trees, glows under a hot blue sky.

If sorrows and fears were brought to Apollo in a song, he would take them away. Music as an expression of the sun-god transforms our darkness into light and meaning.

The laurel wreath was used to crown the victors of athletic and artistic contests. The striving spirit and the crown of victory are both aspects of the sun-god.

Apollo's far-shooting arrows earned him the epithet 'Apollo Longsight', thus implying that he is an image of the part of us which can see the purpose and reason for experiences long before we have emotionally processed them and left them behind.

Here we meet the radiant sun-god Apollo, the gentleman of Olympus and lord of prophecy, music and knowledge. His nickname was Phoebus, which means 'the brilliant', and in myth he delighted in the heights of the mountain peaks. He was the son of Zeus by Leto, the goddess of Night. Unlike other children, Apollo was not nourished on his mother's milk. He was fed nectar and sweet ambrosia, and immediately the newborn baby threw off his swaddling clothes and was endowed with manly vigour. He set forth with the bow and far-shooting arrows which the smith-god Hephaistos had made for him, seeking a place for his sanctuary. But the place he chose was a mountain gorge which formed the lair of the vicious female serpent Python, a beast sent by Hera out of jealousy to destroy Apollo's

THE SUN

mother Leto. The god killed Python with one of his arrows, crowned himself with sacred laurel, and called his new sanctuary Delphi.

At the shrine of Delphi he established his oracle, spoken by a priestess who became known as the Pythoness. Meanwhile, he left Delphi every year in the autumn and travelled to the mysterious land of the Hyperboreans, where he could enjoy an eternally bright sky. Apollo was the enemy of all darkness, and could lift from men the curse of blood-guilt and the toils of sorrow. But he was a tricky deity, for his oracle was double-tongued and elusive, and his arrows could slay not only monsters but also men. Thus he was the god of sudden death as well as being a healer who drove away illness and shadows. Prophecy, normally the gift of the underworld deities, was gradually appropriated by Apollo until he himself became the embodiment of far-reaching vision.

On an inner level, Apollo, the sun-god, is an image of the power of consciousness to dispel the darkness. Like Hecate, who under the name of Artemis was Apollo's twin sister in myth, the god personifies something greater than one individual's capacity to gain knowledge and insight. Apollo is an image of the urge toward consciousness which exists in all life, and therefore he is the natural complement and antithesis to Hecate. Through many long centuries and through the rise and fall of many cultures and civilizations, the thrust toward knowledge and the craving for freedom from the bondage of dark, unknown nature has driven humankind toward impressive although dangerous heights. Apollo represents the spirit of intellectual striving, combined with a vision of the future which encompasses an ideal of perfection.

Thus the Fool's encounter with Apollo the sun-god brings him the hope and clarity of daylight after the long night of waiting in the womb of Hecate. Through many trials and losses the Fool has maintained his goal and his integrity; but the card of the Moon is a dark place where, although the end of the journey is near, the Fool has lost both his confidence and his power of action. But Apollo is the dispeller of fear, and his bright light casts away shadows. The shadows of the Moon are like the night-fears of childhood, where we feel small and unimportant

THE SUN

in the face of the vastness of the unknown, threatened by gigantic shapes that loom in the darkness. Apollo is an image of that hope and faith which spring not from any one person's striving, but from all of us, a human inheritance of nobility and determination which can restore the Fool's faith in himself because it is also a faith in the meaningfulness and purpose of the human journey. The card of the Sun symbolizes that indomitable spirit that has always struggled against superstition, helplessness, ignorance and bondage to fatalism and despair.

It is this spirit which battles with the serpent Python, the embodiment of the negative power of blind instinct and primitive fear. Apollo's music also lifts us out of ourselves, for music speaks with a transpersonal voice, crossing cultures and centuries and embodying human tragedy and triumph. Thus Apollo is a great deity, respected by all the gods, and even the Moirai were once made subject to his will – although only once. But the sun-god too is ambivalent, for too much light too soon can kill if knowledge is premature and destroys the necessary time and darkness for things to gestate. Therefore the card of the Sun follows after the card of the Moon. The burning heat of the sun can scorch, for it does not respect nature's laws. Thus Apollo in myth was often rejected in his advances toward women, for his light was sometimes too bright.

On a divinatory level, the card of Apollo, the sun-god, augurs a time of clarity, optimism and renewed trust. It is possible to understand the pattern, to plan for the future, to move forward. The curses of the night are dispelled, and the Fool is now armed with foresight, purpose and a faith in the striving human spirit. Thus he encounters that great masculine principle in life, working through both men and women, which moves forward toward the goal.

JUDGEMENT

The card of Judgement portrays a young man with curling black hair, dressed in a white tunic and a blood-red travelling cloak. On his head is a winged helmet, and his feet are shod in winged sandals. In his right hand he holds the caduceus, the staff of magic entwined with two snakes. On either side of him, dimly visible, are two columns, one black and one white. The stairs on which he stands ascend to a doorway through which can be glimpsed a rich green landscape over which the sun is just rising. Before him, several carved coffins lie, and from these sarcophagi the dead are rising, reaching out to him as they shrug off their burial shrouds.

The black and white pillars once again reflect the ambivalence of the unconscious with its destructive and creative potentials.

The dead are mummified because the experiences of the past remain unremembered and unchanged in the unconscious, until their meaning suddenly becomes clear.

We can now understand the two snakes entwined around Hermes' staff of magic as emblems of the feminine underworld of the instincts, which Apollo the sun-god conquers but which Hermes relates to in a different way, using it to serve his greater purposes in the design of the journey of life.

Here, as we approach the end of the cycle of the Major Arcana, we meet that god whom we encountered at the beginning – Hermes the Psychopomp, Guide of Souls. In the card of the Magician, Hermes appears as the Fool's inner guide at the beginning of the journey of life – a trickster, a protector of lost travellers, and a magus who can point the way through the uncanny intuitions which in myth the god was said to dispense. Now he is revealed as a powerful underworld deity, emissary of Hades, who summons the dying gently and eloquently by laying his golden staff upon their eyes. But Hermes could also summon the souls of the dead back to life, as

JUDGEMENT

well as ushering them into Hades' realm. In myth, when Tantalos, the king of Lydia, cut his own son in pieces and served them as a feast for the gods, Hermes reassembled the pieces and restored the young man to life. As herald of the heavenly gods, Hermes also freed heroes such as Theseus who had entered Hades' realm illicitly and then got stuck there. He also guided Orpheus into the dark kingdom to seek his lost wife Eurydice, and guided him out again when he had lost her for a second time. Thus Hermes of the card of Judgement is not only Hermes the Guide, but Hermes the Summoner, who leads the souls of the dead to their accounting and prepares them for renewed life.

On an inner level, Hermes the Psychopomp is an image of a process which occurs at certain critical moments in life: a summing-up, when the experiences of the past are gathered together and seen as part of an intelligent pattern, and the consequences of these experiences must be understood and accepted. This process of summing-up is not an intellectual function, but rather a kind of cooking that occurs in the underworld of the unconscious. It is a call for the dead to rise – for the many and varied actions and decisions we perform to knit together and yield a harvest. The artist experiences this process when, after many hours or weeks or even years of attempting to formulate, research, practise technique and give shape to an elusive idea or image, something at last 'happens' and a new creative work is born. This same process can be seen in psychotherapy, where an individual can struggle for many months with the disconnected memories and feelings of the past and present, stuck and blocked, and suddenly a kind of cohesion occurs and one's life pattern makes sense at last. This process can occur in any realm of life where we tunnel blind as moles, pouring effort into something which somehow remains elusive, and at last the effort is rewarded and there is a synthesis and a new development at hand. This is Hermes at his most magical, revealed at last as the true lord of the entirety of the Fool's journey, knitting together through some mysterious process of the intuition the experiences and insights gained from each stage of the journey, and magically blending these to form the beginnings of a new and larger personality.

JUDGEMENT

Thus the figure of Hermes leading the dead souls to judgement embodies a process of birth. It is the birth of a more complete personality, which arises in a nonrational way from the combined experiences of the past, fused by insight and the sense that apparently random events and choices are really secretly connected. The judge of the dead decides what future has been earned from past efforts, and it is on the efforts of the past cards that the Fool's future is built. The card of Judgement symbolizes the rewards for efforts made, although the judge is inside us, not outside in the world. We pay also for our sins of unconsciousness, and reap the harvest of refusing to take up responsibility for our own choices at each stage of the journey. Judgement is an image not just of a new beginning, but a beginning which emerges out of the past. In Eastern philosophy, this is called *karma*. Each person sows seed in his own field, and ultimately must reap the harvest which springs from his own sowing. Although Hermes is often portrayed as a cheat and a liar, here, as Psychopomp, he does not permit the soul to lie. Everything must be accounted for, and the Fool meets at last the consequences of all his choices in life.

On a divinatory level, the card of Judgement, when it appears in a spread, augurs a time when the rewards of past efforts appear. This is a period of summing-up, of a realization of what we have been doing and where we ourselves have created the future which now awaits us. It is an ambiguous card, for it can also imply a disturbing confrontation with all our own evasions and self-betrayals. The reward is not always a pleasant one. The Fool must now answer for his journey, for the time of harvest has arrived, and the mistakes and creative efforts of the past are gathered together to form the future. Whatever occurs to the individual in terms of experiences, the card of Judgement heralds the end of a chapter in life. But unlike the card of Death, it does not imply mourning. Rather, it is a clear perception of the extent to which we have been able to be true to ourselves.

THE WORLD

The card of the World portrays a golden serpent coiled in the shape of an egg, eating its own tail. Within its circumference a strange figure dances, half male and half female, winged, crowned with laurel-leaves, and holding in each hand a golden staff. Around the egg-shape of the serpent can be seen, rising from the clouds, a cup, sword, a flaming wand and a golden pentacle.

The World Snake, called Ouroboros in Greek, was said to be itself both male and female, self-impregnating, self-feeding, immortal and complete. Thus it is the mythic image for both God and nature, here embodied in one symbol.

The four symbols which preside over the realms of water, fire, air and earth reflect the potentials which await development in the new personality.

The golden staffs are connected with the magic wand of Hermes, for the reborn personality can create more potently in the realms of feeling, imagination, mind and matter.

Here we meet Hermaphroditus, who in myth was the child of Hermes and Aphrodite. In one version of the tale, Hermaphroditus was born a double-sexed being. But in another version, this duality or unity was made, rather than born. Hermaphroditus was originally a male child, and to conceal his illicit birth, Aphrodite immediately confided him to the nymphs of Mount Ida, who brought him up in the forests. At the age of fifteen he was a wild and savage youth whose chief pleasure was to hunt in the wooded mountains. One day he arrived at the banks of a limpid lake whose freshness tempted him to bathe. The nymph Salmacis who ruled the lake saw him and was enamoured of his beauty. She told him so, and in vain the shy youth attempted to repulse her. Salmacis threw her arms around him and covered him with kisses. He continued to resist, and

THE WORLD

the nymph cried out, 'O gods! grant that nothing may ever separate him from me, or me from him!' Immediately their two bodies were united and became as one.

The four devices which surround the image of Hermaphroditus in the card of the World belong to the four deities: Aphrodite the love-goddess, Zeus the king of the gods, Athene the goddess of wisdom, and Poseidon the god of earthquakes. We have already encountered these symbols in the card of the Magician: the cup of love, the wand of creative imagination, the sword of the intellect, and the pentacle of physical reality. We will meet these four objects again when we explore the four Suits of the Minor Arcana. The serpent which surrounds Hermaphroditus is the ancient World Snake, which as we have seen embodies the raw instinctual power of life itself, forever devouring and recreating itself.

On an inner level, the image of Hermaphroditus is an image of the experience of being whole. Male and female are more than sexual identifications limited to the genital organs. They are great polarities which encompass all the opposites in life. The double-sexed being, born in one version of the myth and made in another, is a symbol of the potential integration of the opposites within the personality. In one sense Hermaphroditus is born thus, because the potential for this integration is inherent in all of us. But in another sense, Hermaphroditus is made, because it is the varied experiences of the entire journey of the Major Arcana which lead ultimately to this complete being. The qualities of maternal care and paternal ethics, intuition and physical expression, mind and feeling, relationship and solitude, conflict and harmony, spirit and body – all these opposites which war within us and create such struggle in our lives are in this card portrayed as joined, living in harmony within the great circle of the World Snake which is an image of inexhaustible life.

The image of wholeness as it is portrayed in the card of the World is an ideal goal, rather than something which we can completely possess. We are human and therefore imperfect, and the divine androgyne is beyond our reach. But we may glimpse this state whenever there is a

THE WORLD

sense of inner healing, where two warring parts of ourselves have at last come together and some inner resolution has brought peace. Ordinarily, when we encounter these opposites in life and in ourselves, we deny that such a conflict exists, repressing half of it and casting it into the underworld of the unconscious. Or we project the uncomfortable half on to another person, or something in the outside world, and expend our energy battling with something which is really within ourselves. The state of ambivalence is part of the human condition; yet how many of us have the courage to admit our ambivalence? 'Of course I want to get married!' we say, or, 'Of course I want a child!' or 'Of course I love you!' or 'Of course I believe in God!' or 'Of course I love my work!' But as human beings we are complex, and the Fool's journey is really a journey of discovery through the opposites of one's being, conscious and unconscious together. The card of the World is the final card of the Major Arcana, and the end of the Fool's journey. Yet it is also an egg which implies the seed of a new journey. Thus, whenever we feel we have 'arrived' and there is a moment of achievement and healing, a fresh challenge arises, a fresh discovery of the ancient spiralling journey. Thus we continue to grow and change, always moving toward Hermaphroditus, the image of wholeness, yet never achieving it save in a small and sometimes subtle way.

On a divinatory level, the card of the World when it appears in a spread augurs a time of achievement and integration. This is a period of triumph at the successful conclusion of a matter, or the reaching of a goal which has been worked hard for. But this peak is merely a glimpse of something mysterious and elusive, and the dancing Hermaphroditus becomes the foetus who eventually emerges from the cave as the Fool. Thus the great cycle of the Major Arcana ends where it begins, for we might start with Hermaphroditus as the unborn potential of the personality which ultimately leads to the birth of the Fool. And so the circle, like the World Snake, is complete.

THE MINOR ARCANA

The Four Suits

The four Suits of the Tarot – symbolized by the cup, the wand, the sword and the pentacle – are descriptions, in pictorial form, of experiences in four different dimensions or spheres of life. Like the ancient four elements of Greek philosophy, from which it was once believed that all manifest things were made, the four Suits encompass every facet of life's experiences. In a sense, they unfold in greater detail and on a more personal level the archetypal journey portrayed by the twenty-two cards of the Major Arcana. Each Suit focuses on some particular facet of the overall cycle and examines it through many different and detailed phases of development.

Each Suit of the Minor Arcana may be divided into two groups: the numbered cards, of which there are ten in each Suit, and the court cards, of which there are four in each Suit. Through the numbered cards we may glimpse the ordinary experiences of life which come to meet us through events, transactions with others, and through passing states of mind or feeling. Each of the numbered cards reflects a typical, or archetypal, experience, and sooner or later during the course of life we find ourselves standing in each one of these little landscapes. Thus the numbered cards are most commonly interpreted from a divinatory point of view, as reflections of events or happenings in the outer world, although they are really just as 'psychological' as the cards of the Major Arcana.

The court cards which belong to each Suit – Page, Knight, Queen and King – differ from the numbered cards because they do not really describe typical events or experiences. Rather, they embody character types, or dimensions of a particular sphere of life which can be portrayed as human figures. Although they appear as a hierarchy, in reality they are equal in value, but their differing degrees of worldly power indicate their differing degrees of consolidation in the outer world. The Pages in all four Suits of the Minor Arcana are images of the young, delicate beginnings of the qualities of the particular Suit. In other words, this is the raw stuff of that sphere of life in its most juvenile, fragile and incipient form, needing care and protection for its qualities to develop fully. The Knights in all four Suits are images of the volatile, energetic, adolescent phase of the qualities of the particular Suit. This is the youthful, questing and energetic spirit that makes us want to explore and experiment with a particular sphere of life. The Queens in all four Suits are images of the stable, receptive, containing qualities of the particular Suit. Here the energy and aspiration no longer flow out with such abandon into the environment – psychology might call it 'acting out' – but rather, are held within, banked, concentrated and focused, so that greater power might emerge. Here one's values are formed, embodied in the only feminine figures of the court cards. The Kings in all four Suits are images of the dynamic, outgoing, directive qualities of the particular Suit. These powerful masculine figures represent the full use of the energies of this sphere of life in building and concretizing in the outer world.

The archetypal characters of the court cards do not describe qualities which are limited to just men or just women, although the images are definitely sexed. Rather, these masculine and feminine faces imply directive or receptive qualities of energy: masculine and feminine on a deeper level, and available to both men and women. These figures are greater than the numbered cards of the Minor Arcana, yet not so all-encompassing and profound as the figures of the Major Arcana. They fall somewhere in between. The Queen of Pentacles, for example, shares some of the earthy qualities of the Empress, Demeter; yet Demeter is greater because she is not only earthly, but embodies all the vast and fathomless dimensions of the World Mother. The Queen of Cups shares some of the intuitive attributes of both the High Priestess and the Moon; but these latter are greater, because the depths of the unconscious contain more than just the intuitions and passionate feelings embodied by the Queen of Cups.

The court cards contain their own mystery, because they often enter one's life not only as an inner experience, but as actual people. Here we return to the enigma of what psychology calls synchronicity, because when something is ripe for development inside us then often we meet it in the world outside; and when we are on our way to becoming a certain kind of person and need to develop certain inner qualities, frequently just such a person will appear 'outside' as a catalyst from whom we can learn more about ourselves. Many relationships come into our lives because the other person embodies something which we in time must learn to internalize. Thus the court cards span the realms of both psyche and matter in a disturbing way, because these character types may enter our lives as people, in addition to describing qualities we ourselves are in process of developing.

The Suit of Cups corresponds to the ancient element of water, from which, it was said, all life emerged. Water is fluid, without shape, changeable and elusive, yet as real and powerful in its own way as solid rock. The rhythms and depths of the sea are both beautiful and dangerous. So too is the world of feeling, for although feelings change and take their coloration from the shape of the situation surrounding them, yet they have their own rhythm and reality and their own kind of power. The fourteen cards which belong to the Suit of Cups describe the development of feelings through life, the typical ways in which our emotions change and deepen through characteristic human experiences and the catalyst of other people, and the types of character which embody the world of feeling in its purest form. The symbol of the cup has always been associated with the heart, for the fluid which it contains is the fluid world of feeling. Whether this be the clear water of spiritual love or the blood-red wine of passion, the cup from which we drink is the vessel through which we experience relationship.

The Suit of Wands corresponds to the ancient element of fire, which, it was said, emerged spontaneously from nothing and could alter and transform everything it touched without itself being changed. Fire is volatile, a shape-changer, neither solid nor liquid, but a catalyst which reduces objects to their most basic components and transforms their nature. So too is the world of the creative imagination, which can make images out of nothing, and which transforms objects in the 'real' concrete world by infusing them with meaning and significance. Yet the imagination itself remains ungraspable. The symbol of the wand is related to the staff of the magician, who through the mysterious power of the imagination can conjure things into being and perceive connections which the ordinary mind cannot see. The fourteen cards which belong to the Suit of Wands describe the development of the creative imagination and the challenges which it meets in the outer world; the uses to which it can be put, and the dangers of too much imagination without common sense; and the typical characters who embody the realm of the imagination most purely.

The Suit of Swords corresponds to the ancient element of air, which, being invisible, was believed to be the breath of spirit which conceived the idea of creation before it was made manifest. The abode of heaven was the seat of Zeus, king of the gods, from which he formulated his laws and dispensed his plan for the evolution of man. Thus the element of air symbolizes the realm of mind, the faculties of conceptualization and abstract thought which must precede any act of creation and which give structure and meaning to life. The sword with its double cutting edge is a fitting image for the ambivalent power of the mind, which can penetrate the darkest and most incomprehensible object or situation with its keenness, yet which can also cut and wound and sever with its inflexible edge. The fourteen cards which belong to the Suit of Swords describe the development of this rational faculty in both its dark and light forms, through the conflicts and quarrels and separations which thoughts and words can provoke, through the clarity and understanding which the mind can offer, and through the characteristic types who embody the realm of mind in its purest form.

The Suit of Pentacles corresponds to the ancient element of earth, the essential clay from which we are formed and to which we must ultimately return. Earth is both our beginning and our end, and the experience of the body is the original reality before any feeling or image or spirit can inhabit it. Earth can be tilled and shaped, houses built, works created, and the business of living requires adjustment to the requirements of our bodies through food, shelter, clothing, and the money which symbolizes worth, value and reward for energy spent. The symbol of the pentacle, the gold coin which bears the five-pointed star of Hermes, god of magic, merchants and the business deal, means money. But money itself is one of the most profound symbols, and is intimately connected with our sense of self-value and the worth we place on what we achieve in life. The pentacle is also a platter upon which food can be served, a container of whatever we create. The fourteen cards which belong to the Suit of Pentacles describe the development of the 'reality function' and the gradual adjustment through life to the requirements, challenges, disappointments and rewards of the material world; as well as the characteristic types who embody the world of earth in its purest form.

We partake of all four elements, declared the ancient philosophers, and in an inner sense we all possess these four different dimensions of life and four different ways of adapting to it. We must all encounter experiences in the four realms, and our experiences are archetypal, that is, they tend to follow certain basic human patterns. The course of human relationships, for example, is a well-trodden path, however much one might feel one is the very first to have ever felt in a particular way. Our heritage of myths, folklore and fairy tales, not to mention the world's great literature and art, presents us with all the typical human situations of love – separation, idealism, disappointment, rejection, conquest, fulfilment, union and loss. Because our experiences in each of the four realms are typical, we will explore each of the numbered cards of the four Suits through a particular myth which runs through all ten cards and which embodies these characteristic experiences. We will explore the four court cards of each Suit through human figures in myth who personify the characteristic types of that Suit. Thus we can examine in detail the essential human patterns of development that occur emotionally, creatively, intellectually and physically.

For the numbered cards of the Suit of Cups, we will consider the myth of Eros and Psyche, for this is an archetypal love story whose progress touches upon all of the main experiences we meet in relationship with others. For the numbered cards of the Suit of Wands we will examine the myth of Jason and the Golden Fleece, for this is an archetypal story of adventure and the triumph of the creative imagination over the limitations of matter. The progress of this story touches upon all of the main experiences we meet during the effort to expand our lives creatively. For the numbered cards of the Suit of Swords we will follow the myth of Orestes and the Curse of the House of Atreus, for this is an archetypal story of the uses and abuses of the mind and the conflicts, quarrels and reconciliations which we encounter through our ethics and our principles. And for the Suit of Pentacles we will investigate the myth of Daedalus through the numbered cards, for this is an archetypal story of the fate of the spirit incarnated in imperfect flesh, and the development of skills and abilities in the world of form.

ACE OF CUPS

TWO OF CUPS

THREE OF CUPS

FOUR OF CUPS

FIVE OF CUPS

SIX OF CUPS

SEVEN OF CUPS

EIGHT OF CUPS

NINE OF CUPS

TEN OF CUPS

THE SUIT OF CUPS

The Numbered Cards

The legend of Eros and Psyche is really the story of the development and maturation of feelings and the capacity to relate to another person. In its own way it is a journey, although unlike the great journey of the Fool through the Major Arcana it is a specialized adventure which circles around the central motif of the human heart.

Psyche (in Greek the word means 'soul') was a princess of such remarkable beauty that the goddess Aphrodite herself was jealous of her. She instructed her son Eros, the god of love, to punish the audacious mortal. Thus, shortly afterwards, an oracle commanded Psyche's father, under threat of terrifying calamity, to conduct his daughter to a lonely rock where she would become the prey of a monster. But the god Eros, when he saw the girl whom he was supposed to carry to her death in the jaws of the monster who awaited below, was so stunned by her beauty that he stumbled and pricked himself on one of his own arrows – those arrows which he used so effectively to bring sudden love to both mortals and gods. So Eros fell in love with the person he had been sent by his mother to destroy.

Trembling but resigned, Psyche was awaiting on her solitary rock the fulfilment of the oracle, when suddenly she felt herself gently lifted by the winds, which carried her to a magnificent palace. When night fell and Psyche was on the verge of sleep, a mysterious being joined her in the darkness, explaining that he was the husband for whom she was destined. She could not see his features, but his voice was soft and his conversation full of tenderness. Their marriage was duly celebrated, but before the return of dawn the strange visitor disappeared, first making Psyche promise never to attempt to see his face.

Psyche was not discontented with her new life. Nothing was lacking, except the constant presence of her delightful husband, who only came to visit her during the dark hours of the night. Her happiness would have continued in this way had not her two sisters – who were devoured with envy – sown the seeds of suspicion in her heart, by

THE SUIT OF CUPS

telling her that her husband must be some hideous monster to thus hide himself from her. They nagged her so much that one night Psyche, despite her promise, rose from the bed she shared with her husband, stealthily lit a lamp, and held it above the mysterious face. Instead of a fearful monster she beheld the most beautiful youth in the world – Eros himself. At the foot of the bed lay his bow and arrows. In her shocked delight Psyche stumbled and pricked herself with one of the arrows, thus finally falling deeply in love with the young god whom previously she had accepted because he had loved her. But her movement caused a drop of scalding oil to fall on the god's bare shoulder. He awakened at once, reproached Psyche for her faithlessness, and immediately vanished.

The palace disappeared at the same time, and poor Psyche found herself on the lonely rock again in the midst of frightening solitude. At first she considered suicide and threw herself into a nearby river, but the waters bore her lightly to the opposite bank. From then on she wandered the world searching for her lost love, pursued by Aphrodite's anger and forced by the goddess to submit to a series of terrible ordeals. She succeeded, however, in overcoming them one by one thanks to the assistance of the creatures of nature – the ants, the birds, the water-reeds. She even had to descend into the underworld, where no living mortal was permitted to go. Finally, touched by the repentance of his unhappy spouse, whom he had never ceased to love and protect, Eros went to Zeus and implored permission for Psyche to rejoin him. Zeus consented and conferred immortality upon Psyche. Aphrodite forgot her rancour, and the second wedding of the two lovers was celebrated on Olympus with great rejoicing.

Ace of Cups

The card of the Ace of Cups portrays a beautiful black-haired woman rising from a foamy sea. She holds up a single golden cup.

In this card we meet that goddess who is the initiator and moving power behind the tale of the love of Eros and Psyche: Aphrodite the Foam-Born, goddess of love in its most noble and its most degraded aspects. In myth, the birth of Aphrodite was a strange one. When, at the instigation of his mother Gaea, the wily Cronos had castrated his heavenly father Uranus, he cast the severed genitals into the sea. They floated on the surface of the waters, producing a white foam out of which rose Aphrodite. Carried on the breath of Zephyrus, the West Wind, the goddess was borne along the coast of Kythera and finally landed on the shores of Cyprus. She was greeted by the Horae, the goddesses of the seasons, who dressed her richly, adorned her with precious jewels, and conducted her to the assembly of the Immortals.

Aphrodite was a complex goddess. The essence of feminine beauty, everything about her was pure charm and harmony. Yet she could be jealous, spiteful, vain, deceitful, treacherous, lazy and vindictive. Throughout all nature she spread her life-bringing joy; yet she was also the fearful divinity who filled human hearts with the frenzy of passion. Those whom Aphrodite chose for her victims were often unfortunate; such would betray their own fathers, or abandon their homes, or would be overcome with incestuous or bestial passions. But the same Aphrodite protected legitimate unions and presided over the sanctity of marriage.

In short, Aphrodite is an image of a force of nature. The meaning of the Aces in all four Suits of the Minor Arcana is an initial eruption of raw energy, and the black-haired goddess emerging from the sea bearing her single golden cup represents an upsurge of raw feeling. This is the urge toward relationship, which must precede any actual encounter with another; for if we are not ready, then the other will not appear. In the tale, Eros and Psyche would never have met, had it not been for Aphrodite; for it is her caprice which inaugurates the action in the story. Thus the Ace of Cups implies the beginning of the great journey through the realm of the heart, where abundance of feeling erupts and drives the individual into a relationship.

On a divinatory level, the Ace of Cups heralds an outpouring of feeling, although this feeling has not yet differentiated and emerges as raw, vital and often overwhelming. The potential is implied for the beginning of a relationship, although often this has not yet manifested. The individual is ready to embark on the journey of love.

Two of Cups

The card of the Two of Cups portrays the initial meeting between Eros and Psyche. Psyche, dressed in white to proclaim her virginity, is bound by the order of Aphrodite on a high rock surrounded by sea. At her feet stands a golden cup. She looks away into the distance, awaiting her certain death in the jaws of the monster who lurks beneath the sea. Behind her, Eros hovers in the sky, shimmering with his golden hair and golden wings. In his right hand he holds a golden cup. In his left hand he carries the arrow with which he has just accidentally pricked himself, thereby inadvertently falling in love with the woman he has been ordered to kill.

The Twos in all four Suits of the Minor Arcana represent a polarization of the initial raw energy of the Aces. Here, in the Two of Cups, that polarization implies the attraction of male and female. The raw feeling which erupted in the Ace has now found an object, and Eros has found another with whom he can fuse. In Plato's ancient fable about the origins of mankind, the human soul was once perfectly spherical and contained both male and female. But this androgynous soul divided, and thus the human race, comprised of men and women, is blindly driven to seek its missing half. To the Greek mind, erotic attraction represented something both sensual and

THE SUIT OF CUPS

spiritual, for as well as providing physical pleasure it was also a seeking of the soul for its own completion.

When any new potential begins to emerge from the unconscious into the life of the individual, it starts first by projecting itself on to something or someone outside. Thus, when the potential for fulfilment implied by the Ace of Cups begins to move within the person, the first indication of this movement is attraction to another. In that other we see a glimpse of what we ourselves are in the process of becoming. In the mortal Psyche, the god Eros sees a chance for humanization, for he is a disembodied spirit of love which has not yet been incarnated in human relationship. In the god Eros, the mortal Psyche eventually – although not yet – sees the potential for immortality, which can lift her human love to a higher and more spiritual level. The Two of Cups introduces us to the protagonists in the tale, and the primal power of Aphrodite has become the power of attraction.

On a divinatory level, the Two of Cups augurs the beginning of a relationship. It can also suggest a reconciliation where an already existing relationship has undergone difficulty or separation. It can even imply the meeting and contractual arrangements of business partners, for here too the element of relationship is invoked.

Three of Cups

The card of the Three of Cups portrays the wedding of Eros and Psyche. Standing on a rock surrounded by water, Psyche faces us dressed in a bridal gown, her hair decked with flowers. She holds a bunch of white lilies. Behind her is the bridegroom whom she cannot yet see – Eros, the radiant god of love, armed with his bow and quiver of golden arrows. Around them in a circle dance three ondines or water nymphs, each rising from the water and holding aloft a golden cup in celebration of the marriage.

The Threes in every Suit of the Minor Arcana represent a stage of initial completion. A new dimension of life is unfolding, and the first part of the journey has now been achieved. The Three of Cups is therefore a card of celebration, representing an experience of emotional fulfilment and the completion of the initial attraction. The couple have come together, and there is a feeling of joy and promise. But the story of Eros and Psyche tells us something quite important about that initial stage of fulfilment and completion. Psyche has not yet seen her bridegroom, nor, in the myth, does she question this lack of true encounter. Initially she is content to live with Eros in a kind of dream-state where he comes to her only at night, under the cover of darkness. Therefore, along with the joy and celebration of this marriage, a certain naiveté lurks. This is the immediately recognizable state of being 'in love', where we are enchanted by our image of the other, but where the real partner has not yet become visible to our eyes. This initial coming together is a joyous experience, a celebration of love and life, an exciting beginning. Much of the world's literature and drama portrays the bliss of just such a state. But the message is: Enjoy it while you can. There is a good deal more to come, both happy and sorrowful, before the journey through the Suit of Cups is complete and the love of Eros and Psyche has emerged with all its human and divine potential. The Three of Cups is an initiation into life, full of promise. The maiden becomes a bride, and leaves behind forever her virginity and her innocence. But this is a card of transition heralding further developments. The journey is not yet finished, and hard work lies ahead.

On a divinatory level, the Three of Cups suggests the celebration of a marriage, the start of a love affair, the birth of a child, or some other situation of emotional fulfilment and promise. But each of these situations is also a beginning, an initiation into deeper levels of the heart's experience, and the herald of further explorations in the future.

Four of Cups

The card of the Four of Cups portrays Psyche, the new bride, seated in the beautiful palace of the god Eros. Through the white columns we can glimpse the sea. To either side of Psyche

THE SUIT OF CUPS

sit her ugly sisters, clothed in red and black gowns. They are whispering to her that her bridegroom must be a dreadful monster; otherwise why would he conceal himself from the light of the sun and visit her only at night? On her face Psyche wears a look of discontent. Before her stand four golden cups.

The Fours in all the Suits of the Minor Arcana are the cards of divine discontent. Although everything seems happy and rewarding, still there is doubt and suspicion. The Four of Cups portrays this discontent on a feeling level. Psyche lives richly and is visited at night by a loving and tender husband, but still she is not satisfied. The jealous, unprepossessing sisters are in a way the inner promptings of Psyche's own soul, for although they are spiteful and negative and cause her to doubt, nevertheless they probe at a real problem: Psyche's blindness and ignorance of who and what her partner truly is. Thus the initial fulfilment of the Three has already proven to be a disappointment, for there is a growing awareness that something is wrong, something is not being dealt with. Each of us has these ugly sisters within us, a kind of shadow side to the personality which means ill yet ultimately yields good, because it forces us to explore more deeply and demand more honesty in our emotional dealings with others. If Psyche had remained in her blind, blissful state of ignorance she would never have grown, and the full potential of both her relationship with Eros and her own self would never be reached. Thus the Four of Cups, the card of discontented feelings and emotional dissatisfaction for no apparent reason, is both negative and positive. It portrays all our mean and petty suspicions and doubts of another; and this forms the seed of all betrayals. Yet it also portrays a mysterious intelligent force at work within the individual which somehow knows there is further to travel.

On a divinatory level, the Four of Cups augurs a time of dissatisfaction, boredom and depression within a relationship. There is a feeling of being let down or cheated, although the one who does the cheating is usually oneself because of one's unreal expectations. This dissatisfaction can lead to long-standing, unexpressed resentment; or it can lead to looking more deeply at the relationship, a harder path because previous assumptions and fantasies will then be challenged.

Five of Cups

The card of the Five of Cups portrays the aftermath of Psyche's betrayal of Eros. Her sisters have stirred her fears to such an extent that she has broken her promise to her husband and lit a lamp to see his sleeping face. Here we see Psyche standing distraught before the empty nuptial couch, the lamp in one hand, the other hand reaching in desperation toward the departing figure of Eros which can be glimpsed disappearing behind the marble columns of their beautiful palace. In the foreground, four cups lie overturned, their contents spilled over the floor. A fifth cup remains standing, still intact, beside them.

The Five of Cups represents that testing time in a relationship when one experiences regret over past actions. This card poses the difficult problem of betrayal, which, as part of the Suit of Cups, is presented as a necessary and potentially creative experience. Although it is painful, betrayal breaks the magical blind cocoon of being 'in love' and totally merged with another, for to betray can sometimes mean being oneself. Psyche's betrayal is not done out of thoughtlessness or greed; it springs from her urge to know her partner, and the god is in some ways wrong to deny her this knowledge. Thus it is an honest act, provoking inevitable conflict which nevertheless is necessary because any other action would constitute a self-betrayal.

Betrayal of another's unreasonable demand or expectation is a difficult but frequent aspect of the deepening of relationship. The lover, husband or wife who says, 'Do not seek to really know me, but remain in love with the image I want you to have', will invoke betrayal, and the betrayer, like Psyche, must often suffer the consequences. But the presence of one intact cup in the image tells us that all is not lost; something remains to build upon. Psyche now knows who her husband is, and she knows that she loves him, not her fantasy of him.

Without this rite of passage she would have been stuck in the anxiety and resentment of the Four of Cups. Now she suffers regret, but there is something remaining to work with.

On a divinatory level, the Five of Cups implies regret over past actions. Something has gone wrong, a betrayal has occurred, and there is sadness and remorse. Separation in a relationship can occur. But this card does not augur a final ending. Something remains which can be worked on, and it is up to the individual to take up the challenge and make the commitment to the future.

Six of Cups

The card of the Six of Cups portrays Psyche seated on a rock, behind which a calm sea can be seen. In her left hand she holds a golden cup, into which she pensively stares. In her right hand she holds the rather bedraggled remains of her bridal bouquet of white lilies. Around her on the rocky ledges stand five more golden cups.

The Six of Cups is a card of nostalgia. Here we see Psyche abandoned; her mysterious husband has flown away, the beautiful palace in which they lived has vanished, and she has nothing left but her pleasant memories. However, despite this catastrophe, Psyche appears tranquil, for the Six of Cups is not an unhappy card. Through the past, Psyche has gained something very precious. She has truly seen Eros, and now knows that she loves him for himself rather than for the comfort and pleasure he has provided. Thus, despite her loss, she knows something about herself, and it is this truth which fosters the harmony we see in the card.

The stillness and serenity which often occur after a crisis in our lives are related to this stage in the story. Here the unreal dreams and expectations of the past, through testing and disappointment, somehow crystallize into something solid and real. Psyche has taken up the challenge of regaining her lost love after the regrets and remorse of the

Five of Cups, and is therefore at peace with herself. Her love has become reality; thus she has something to build upon. The nostalgia of the past always comes back to haunt us at such times, but there is a nugget of truth in it. It is not merely sentimental fantasy without foundation. After the self-recrimination of the Five, the Six of Cups represents a positive turn in Psyche's journey toward her goal.

On a divinatory level, the Six of Cups augurs a time of serenity which grows out of the testing of the dreams of the past. Sometimes an old love from the past returns, or a cherished dream which one has held in the past seems possible of fruition in the near future. The blind 'in love' state has solidified, and although the past may seem beautiful and irrevocably lost, something of its promise emerges, tempered and strengthened, into the present. This card implies nostalgia about the past, but with a difference: The past can lead to the future, and the dream is experienced as still possible, even near achievement.

Seven of Cups

The card of the Seven of Cups portrays the goddess Aphrodite confronting Psyche with the tasks which she must perform in order to win Eros back. Psyche kneels on a rock before the goddess, acknowledging the divine sovereignty in all matters of love. Aphrodite, rising out of the water, points to seven golden cups which float on the clouds before her.

The Seven of Cups represents the boon – and problem – of being confronted with too many possibilities in matters of the heart. This is the card of 'castles in the air'. The intuition perceives all kinds of potentials for the future, but these visions of possibilities must be made real and concrete by a great deal of hard work. Psyche has risen from her nostalgic reflection, portrayed in the Six of Cups, with a firm commitment to her love, and she humbly prays to Aphrodite for aid, although she now knows full well that the

THE SUIT OF CUPS

capricious goddess is the initiator of all her catastrophic changes in fortune. Aphrodite, in response, guarantees the future reunion with Eros, and so happy fantasies of the resolution of the relationship are invoked. For Psyche, anything is now possible. But Aphrodite demands a price: hard labours which take time and gruelling effort, care and forethought, and which carry the risk of humiliation and suffering. But Psyche cannot have Eros without performing these labours.

The uprush of happy fantasies of a marvellous future where anything is possible in love is a natural outgrowth of the inner commitment which has taken place in the Six. When we have achieved a deep realization of our true feelings, or have connected with an important part of ourselves as Psyche has with her love for Eros, the future opens up as a rosy vision. 'Now I know what it has really been for', we say confidently, because we now know that the possibilities are endless. But time and careful choice and hard work are now necessary to make those possibilities a concrete reality. The deep and honest relationship which Psyche now knows she wants promises a happy future. But she must first accept the limitations of reality: that her husband is still too immature to accept such honesty, and that she herself must learn patience, faith and perseverance before she can win him back.

On a divinatory level, the Seven of Cups augurs an emotional situation where many potentials are evident, but where the individual is faced with the challenge of choosing and acting in realistic terms to make those potentials manifest.

Eight of Cups

The card of the Eight of Cups portrays Psyche performing the final task Aphrodite has given her: the journey into the underworld to bring back a pot of Persephone's beauty cream. Psyche is shown empty-handed, descending the steps into the darkness of the underworld, her face set in sadness and resignation because she realizes that she will probably not survive the journey. Behind her, abandoned, stand eight neatly stacked golden cups.

THE SUIT OF CUPS

The Eight of Cups represents the most difficult stage of Psyche's journey toward her goal of relationship: the voluntary giving up of hope for the future. No living mortal can descend into Hades' realm, and as far as Psyche is concerned, this final task that Aphrodite has set must mean death. Nevertheless she obeys the goddess, for she is loyal to her commitment to love. Thus it is a letting go of hope. All the tasks so meticulously performed, suggested by the eight neatly stacked cups, have been to no avail. She sees the situation as it truly is – that Aphrodite will never relent – and so in despair she turns her back and walks away from her past hopes.

This stage of relationship is one of the most painful, because it means that there is nothing further that can be done. Increased efforts avail nothing; we must give up and start again. Many people, when confronted with the dilemma reflected by the Eight of Cups, refuse to acknowledge the impasse, and continue to plead, bully, bludgeon or blackmail the partner in the hope of a response which is no longer possible in the present circumstances. The underworld, as we saw in the Major Arcana card of Death, is a symbol of mourning and the relinquishing of control; it is the place of the death and transformation of our old attitudes. Therefore, when nothing furthers, we must be willing to let go, not as a kind of 'deal' to guarantee a future reconciliation – for that is not true relinquishing – but because we can do nothing else. This is a bowing to what seems like fate, an acceptance of an ending. Whatever happens, this letting go will change us, because it is a submission to that which is greater – not the wilfulness of the partner, but the will of the divine, imaged here as the great goddess of love.

On a divinatory level, the Eight of Cups implies the necessity of giving something up. The truth of the situation must be faced; no further action will avail, and there is no way to go except to let go. Often this is accompanied by depression, for the underworld is a place of mourning. The future cannot be manipulated; we go empty-handed into the unknown.

Nine of Cups

The Nine of Cups portrays the moment of joy when Psyche is rescued from the darkness of the underworld and reunited with Eros. Psyche and Eros stand face to face embracing, garlanded with flowers, on a rock rising from the sea. Each holds a golden cup. Beside them Aphrodite stands benignly, raising a cup in blessing on their union. Below them, are six golden cups carefully stacked in celebration of the restored lovers.

The Nine of Cups is the wish-card, representing satisfaction and the fulfilment of an emotional dream. Psyche and Eros are at last reunited in honest love for each other, standing face to face. Each has betrayed the other; each knows on a profound level who the partner is; and they have understood and forgiven each other. Because of this, the capricious Aphrodite blesses the union, for the power of unconditional human love can sway even the gods. This ecstatic moment of fulfilment, unlike the initial celebration of the Three of Cups, has been truly earned, not by force or will or emotional manipulation, or the covert bullying of loudly announced self-sacrifice, but by the steady inner commitment of the only mortal in the story. Throughout, Psyche has done what she has done through loyalty to her own feeling. Thus she has earned the right to claim her divine husband and puts even the gods to shame.

This second meeting is the real marriage of Eros and Psyche, suggesting what such a union can be. It arises not out of falling in love but from a commitment to loving including resentment, betrayal, separation, despair and readiness to give it up if required. This is rare, for the journey of the Cups is not about falling in love and living happily ever after, and then walking away when the beloved proves to be a disappointment. It is really an inner journey toward a commitment to one's own feeling values, and thus is an inner as well as an outer union.

On a divinatory level, the Nine of Cups heralds a time of pleasure and satisfaction, and the fulfilment of a cherished wish. It represents the reward for efforts made, and the validation of one's commitment.

Ten of Cups

The card of the Ten of Cups portrays the raising of Psyche to divine status, so that she may enter the world of the gods with her husband. The couple stand once again in Eros' beautiful palace, hands linked. Psyche no longer wears her virginal white gown; she is clothed now in shimmering gold, and on her shoulders, like her husband, bears a pair of golden wings. Before them stand ten golden cups.

The Ten of Cups represents a state of permanence and ongoing contentment. The ecstasy of the reunion of the lovers in the Nine of Cups has not dissipated, as did the celebration of the Three into the discontent of the Four, for this marriage is built upon a conscious union of two loving but separate partners. Thus they can enjoy a future which will withstand any challenges offered by life or by the gods.

That Psyche is raised to immortal status implies that her love for Eros now encompasses not only a personal, sensual dimension, but a spiritual one as well. Eros has been humanized by Psyche's love; he no longer needs to hide his face from her sight. Psyche, on the other hand, experiences that sense of connectedness with the divine which deep love can sometimes bring. It is sometimes said that loving another person opens the heart to loving life itself; life has meaning and purpose, and a larger, brighter world appears before one's vision. Plato once wrote that when we look into the face of the beloved, we see there the reflection of the god to whose choir we once belonged. It is as though love, when it has passed through many tests and been built upon honesty and humility, connects us with our own souls, and with a feeling of permanence, meaning and rightness in life. This is the promise inherent in the Ace of Cups, which culminates in the Ten. Not every relationship can achieve it, and no relationship can achieve it all the time. Yet we humans seem to go on trying.

On a divinatory level, the Ten of Cups augurs ongoing contentment and permanence in the realm of the heart.

THE SUIT OF CUPS

The Court Cards

Page of Cups

The card of the Page of Cups portrays a boy of around twelve years old, black haired and wearing a pale lilac tunic, kneeling at the edge of a deep blue pool. On the ground beside the pool stands a golden cup, into which the youth peers ardently, for he is studying the reflection of his own face and is struck by its beauty. Around him grow clumps of irises and narcissi, budding, not yet in bloom. A woodland landscape screens a gentle blue sky.

The court cards of the Suit of Cups are represented by mythic figures who embody the typical characteristics of the Suit. Here, in the card of the Page of Cups, we meet the changeable, vulnerable, gentle beginnings of the element of water: the nascent emergence of the capacity to feel. This is embodied in the mythic figure of the beautiful youth Narcissus, who fell in love with his own reflection in the water. Narcissus was a Thespian, the son of the river-god Cephisus by a nymph. Anyone might excusably have fallen in love with Narcissus, even as a child, and his path was indeed strewn with ardent suitors of both sexes who were enamoured of the boy's beauty. But his mother, on the advice of the seer Tiresias, had never permitted the boy to see his own reflection. Thus he was quite unaware of his own identity.

THE SUIT OF CUPS

One day when wandering the Thespian countryside, Narcissus came upon a pool. This pool was fed by a spring, clear as silver, and had never yet been disturbed by cattle, birds, wild beasts, men, or even by branches dropping off the trees that shaded it. As the boy cast himself down, exhausted, on the grassy verge to slake his thirst, he fell in love with his reflection. At first he tried to embrace and kiss the beautiful boy who confronted him, but presently recognized himself, and lay gazing enraptured into the pool, hour after hour.

At length Narcissus could no longer bear the agony of this unobtainable love. He plunged his dagger into his breast, crying, 'Ah, youth, beloved in vain, farewell!' as he expired. His blood soaked the earth, and up sprang the white narcissus flower with its red corollary.

Narcissus, the Page of Cups, seems at first to be merely an image of vain self-love. But he may also be seen as an image of self-discovery, for loving another must spring first from recognition and value of oneself; otherwise it is a sad and often fruitless exercise in seeking in the other what one has not yet discovered within. Such relationships tend to be doomed, and the apparent selfishness of Narcissus is really the beginning of a discovery of one's own worthiness of being loved. This is often the start of a genuine capacity to love another as a separate person, rather than a potential supplier of qualities one needs to feel complete.

Thus Narcissus, the Page of Cups, is an ambiguous figure. In one sense, the Page of Cups, as an image of the gentle, nascent beginnings of the feeling-life, suggests the birth of something new – a capacity for love, or the renewal of faith in love which might previously have been damaged or bruised from an unfortunate relationship. Then the sense of self-love which Narcissus embodies is the beginning of healing, vain and infantile though it might seem at the time. Many people, after a shattering separation or loss of a loved one, spend a long time in a kind of emotional twilight, where they feel they have nothing to give anyone. Often during such a time, one does not care much for oneself either. But the gentle, delicate stirrings of this renewal of the capacity to love often take the form of a slow and gradual interest in oneself – one's body, one's environment, trying to please and feed oneself with things that bring pleasure rather than pain or reminders of pain. This is a process which must occur before the individual is ready to risk another emotional encounter. The Page of Cups, like the other Pages in the Minor Arcana, suggests something fragile and delicate, easily misunderstood and easily crushed. So too is our nascent sense of self-love which can ultimately lead to a more fulfilling relationship life. We can easily call Narcissus callous and selfish, because he has eyes for no other than himself. But he must begin with himself before he can see anyone else – and it is interesting to note that in the myth it is his mother who tries to keep him from self-knowledge and self-recognition.

The rather sad ending of the story of Narcissus can also be taken on several levels. In some ways, the Page of Cups and all that he embodies must eventually transform – or 'die' – before love of another can fully develop. But it is necessary that this be a self-sacrifice, a genuine moving from self-preoccupation to awareness of others. Thus in a way it is fitting and right that Narcissus end his own existence, for he transforms into the Knight of Cups, where the feeling-life can now move freely outward toward others.

When the Page of Cups appears in a spread, the birth of something new on the feeling level is suggested. This might be a new relationship, a new quality of feeling within a relationship, even the birth of a child. Often the Page of Cups augurs a renewal of the capacity to love, beginning with love of self, after a time of hurt and withdrawal. This delicate quality must be nurtured or it can rapidly vanish.

Knight of Cups

The card of the Knight of Cups portrays a pale-skinned, beautiful young man with black hair and soulful eyes, mounted on an elegant white horse. He is dressed in a violet tunic and silver fish-scale armour, and wears a silver helmet crowned with a silver fish's tail. He leads his horse gracefully across a bubbling stream where fish leap from the water. Around him lies a romantic landscape of woods and green hills, while in the distance the sea can be glimpsed beneath a pale blue sky. In one hand the Knight holds a golden cup.

THE SUIT OF CUPS

Here, in the card of the Knight of Cups, we meet the volatile, sensitive, changeable dimension of the element of water, which like the stream is full of life and always moving. This is embodied by the mythic hero Perseus, who is motivated on all his adventures by love of women, and must on his journeys confront the many faces of the feminine, both dark and light, before he can be united with his love. Perseus was the son of Zeus by a mortal woman called Danae, to whom the god appeared as a shower of gold. Danae's father Acrisius had been warned by the Delphic Oracle that his daughter would bear a son who would kill him, so he shut Danae and her infant up in a chest which he cast into the sea. Protected by the water-deities, they were washed ashore at Seriphos and taken under the protection of King Polydectes. But Polydectes fell in love with Danae, and pursued her all through the years of Perseus' childhood and adolescence. Eventually Polydectes resolved to kill Perseus because the young man opposed the match, believing his mother deserved something better. So the king therefore sent the young man on an apparently hopeless quest, to obtain the head of the terrible Gorgon Medusa.

Perseus was favoured by goddesses each step of the way. The Graeae, three old crones who shared only one eye between them and who knew the secrets of the future, told him where to find the she-monster, and Athenen provided the young hero with a magic shield. Thus Perseus was able to slay the Gorgon by watching her reflection in the mirror of the shield, in order to protect his mother. He took the head of the Gorgon with him and on his way back to Seriphos he passed through Ethiopia, and had to rescue the beautiful maiden Andromeda from the clutches of a sea-monster. He killed the monster, freed the girl, and married her. Then he returned to Seriphos, killed Polydectes who meanwhile had attempted to assault Danae, and set forth with his mother and his bride to the place of his birth, where his grandfather Acrisius had once tried to murder him. Although he did not deliberately seek vengeance against Acrisius, he accidentally killed him, and thus became king of Argos. But the place held sad memories for him, so he travelled to Tiryns, where he founded a glorious house.

THE SUIT OF CUPS

Perseus, the Knight of Cups, is an image of the true romantic spirit, the champion of women in distress, the worshipper of love, beauty and truth, and the defender of high ideals who ceaselessly searches for that perfect love which ultimately exists only in the spirit yet which always seems to be around the next corner in the next beloved. The romantic spirit of the Knight of Cups embodies all that is gentle, idealistic, and kind, although he is not a weak character and is capable of sacrificing everything in the name of his ideal or his beloved. This is in a sense a picture of the state of being 'in love', an experience which every realist may claim dies rapidly with the familiarity of marriage, children and family obligations, but which every romantic believes can and ought to remain forever. When it does not, the Knight of Cups may move on, still seeking the ultimate experience of holy love. The holiness of the Knight of Cups does not, of course, preclude sex. But sexual relationships for this figure must be blended with love and a kind of ecstasy of the spirit. 'Mere' bodily satisfaction does not interest him. Historically, the ideals of courtly love which flourished in the Middle Ages reflect the spirit of the Knight of Cups. The young knight always worshipped his beloved from afar; he would not sully her with base desires, but wrote poetry to her and often offered his life to protect her.

Perseus is different from other heroes precisely because of this high idealism and worship of women. Unlike such figures as Heracles, who meets his challenges because he is attempting to expiate a sin, or Theseus, who meets them because they are exciting, Perseus follows his fate because of love – primarily, at first, love of his mother. This quality of worshipping and idealizing the mother is characteristic of the Knight of Cups, for despite his strength he kneels at the feet of a queen – a woman higher and more powerful than he. The quality of love represented by the Knight of Cups often contains this element of worshipping someone before whom one feels slightly unworthy – or someone who already has a husband. It is not yet a love of equals; that we must meet later in the Queen and King of Cups. But it is, in its fashion, love, and should not be mocked as adolescent or immature. Without the Knight of Cups, we would live in a bleak and colourless world indeed.

THE SUIT OF CUPS

When the Knight of Cups appears in a spread, it is time for the individual to experience this heady and romantic dimension of love. Often the Knight augurs a proposal of marriage, or an experience of falling in love. Sometimes, on another level, he implies an artistic proposition, a relationship of another kind which is no less exalted and idealistic. Or he may enter one's life as a poetic and sensitive young man – a herald of one's own emerging romanticism.

Queen of Cups

The card of the Queen of Cups portrays a pale, mysteriously beautiful woman with long, rich black hair, wearing a blue-green gown and a golden crown. She is seated on a golden throne whose arms are engraved with golden snakes. Her robes trail into a deep blue pool at her feet. In one hand she holds a golden apple; in the other, a golden cup into which she peers with a look of profound concentration. Behind her, beyond rich green fields, can be glimpsed a deep blue sea beneath a vivid sky.

Here, in the card of the Queen of Cups, we meet, the stable, containing, introverted depths of the element of water – the private inner world of feeling which is bottomless and ultimately unfathomable. This is embodied in the mythic figure of Helen, whom we met in the Major Arcana card of the Lovers, and whose beauty was so great that the Trojan War began because of her. Helen was the child of Zeus by Leda, and when she grew to womanhood at the palace of her foster-father King Tyndareos of Sparta, all the princes of Greece came with rich gifts as her suitors. Eventually she married Menelaus, who became king of Sparta after the death of Tyndareos. But the marriage was doomed to failure, for Aphrodite promised Paris, the Trojan prince, the most beautiful woman in the world if he awarded the goddess the prize in the beauty contest which we encountered in the card of the Lovers; and Helen was that woman.

In due course Paris and Helen met and fell in love, and Helen eloped

THE SUIT OF CUPS

with him, the result of which insult to King Menelaus was the Trojan War in which Paris was killed. But Helen's beauty eventually attracted her three more lovers – not to mention the hero Theseus, who abducted her when she was only an adolescent. These later lovers were all men who won her favours while she was held behind Trojan walls, so Helen enjoyed an eventful ten years of war. When the Trojans had been defeated, Menelaus went to seek Helen, whom he had sworn to kill for her adultery. But at the sight of her beauty he fell in love all over again, and brought her back to Sparta. Whether she remained faithful to Menelaus for her remaining years is a question which myth does not answer.

Helen, the Queen of Cups, is more than an image of alluring feminine beauty. She embodies the hypnotic power of the feminine world of the feelings, a power which is magical and magnetic and defies a mere physical perfection. Throughout Helen's story, countless men pursue her; yet we never really know from the tales what Helen herself wanted, or what sort of woman she really was. It is as though she herself is water, and all men see in her the reflection of the depths of their own souls. She is a cypher, a mystery, motivated by her own secret purposes and feelings. She might be taken as a whore, since she apparently offers her favours to so many men – some of them enemies of her own homeland. Yet we are left with the feeling that, passionate though she might be, Helen does nothing that she does not wish to do. Even her choice of husband is indeed a free choice, for in the story she indicated her favouring of Menelaus by placing a wreath on his head – an unusual thing for a woman of the time, who was usually forced to marry whomever her father or brothers wanted her to. When she tires of Menelaus, she fearlessly pursues her great love adventure with Paris, rather than resorting to coy clandestine meetings. Whomever she loves, Helen gives herself to wholeheartedly. She conquers men without trying, because she is the embodiment of all the secret unconscious fantasies of the perfect woman that men have attempted to articulate over the ages. The figure of Helen is both virginal and harlot, a calculator and a victim. In short, she is a mass of paradoxes, for although the logic of the heart is unarguable, yet it defies rational analysis, and often flies in the face of morality. The Queen of Cups is elusive as a character, yet she stirs up trouble wherever she goes, activating the depths in others and inaugurating action and conflict without doing anything at all. Thus she may be seen as an image of the unconscious, pursuing its secret purposes unbeknownst to the conscious mind, yet luring the individual into crisis and conflict and intense passion and fate through its mysterious seductive power.

When the Queen of Cups appears in a spread, it is time for the individual to encounter the deep, unknowable, paradoxical world of feeling in himself or herself. The Queen of Cups may enter one's life as a mysterious, hypnotic woman, not necessarily overtly seductive yet strangely disturbing, and a catalyst for the emergence of deep feelings and fantasies which have previously been hidden from awareness. She may appear as a beloved or as a rival, but either way such an encounter is not mere chance. It is rather an augury for the emergence of these soul qualities within the individual. For the woman who is unaware of the Helen in herself and identifies with the maternal or practical sides of feminity, the Queen of Cups implies that it is time to meet her, even if the catalyst is the 'other woman'. For the man who is unaware of the depths of his own soul, and bases his reality on rational thought and concrete facts, the Queen of Cups heralds a deepening and development of the inner life, whether or not the catalyst is an actual woman.

King of Cups

The card of the King of Cups portrays a pale, black-haired and black-bearded man with large, sympathetic dark eyes, dressed in a deep blue robe and wearing a golden crown. He is seated on a golden throne whose arms are engraved with golden crabs. In one hand he holds a golden cup; in the other, a lyre. At his feet, steps descend to the water of a harbour, out of which a crab can be seen emerging. Behind him, beyond the promontory of land on which his throne stands, a turbulent sea can be glimpsed.

THE SUIT OF CUPS

Here, in the card of the King of Cups, we meet the active, dynamic dimension of water, which overtly seeks to form relationships and even to guide and help others. This is embodied in the mythic figure of Orpheus, the singer, who was both priest and healer, yet whose own story is sad and lonely although he brought comfort to his fellows. Orpheus was the son of the Thracian King Oeagrus and the Muse Calliope, and he was the most famous poet and musician who ever lived. Apollo presented him with a lyre and the Muses taught him its use, so that he not only enchanted the wild beasts, but made even the trees and rocks move from their places to follow the sound of his music. He joined the Argonauts on their quest for the Golden Fleece, and his music helped them to overcome many difficulties. On his return, he married Eurydice, and settled in Thrace.

But his life was not destined to be happy. One day a man tried to assault Eurydice in the valley of the River Peneius, and she trod on a serpent as she fled and died of its bite. But Orpheus boldly descended into the underworld, hoping to fetch her back. He not only charmed the ferryman Charon, the three-headed dog Cerberus and the three Judges of the Dead with his plaintive music, but temporarily suspended the tortures of the damned, and so far soothed the dark heart of Hades that he won leave to restore Eurydice to the upper world. But Hades made one condition: that Orpheus might not look behind him until she was safely back in the light of the sun. Eurydice followed Orpheus up through the dark passages, guided by the sound of his lyre. But at the last moment he lost his trust, and looked back to see whether she was still there; and so he lost her forever.

After this Orpheus took up the role of a priest, teaching the mysteries and preaching the evil of sacrificial murder to the men of Thrace. But the god Dionysos grew jealous of him because his fame spread and men began to worship him as though he were divine. The god set his mad maenads upon Orpheus, and they tore him to pieces in their frenzy. The Muses tearfully collected his limbs and buried them at the foot of Mount Olympus, where the nightingales now sing more sweetly than anywhere else in the world.

THE SUIT OF CUPS

Orpheus, the King of Cups, is an image of the wounded healer, the figure who through compassion and empathy can heal others yet who cannot heal his own hurt in the realm of the heart. In many ways he is the ancient equivalent of many modern social workers and psychotherapists – the individual who longs to be in touch with the world of feeling, and tries constantly to help others to relate, yet who sometimes lacks trust in his or her own personal life and therefore cannot ultimately achieve the fulfilling relationship which is so desired. The King of Cups places human relationship and human love above everything, and will go to great lengths to initiate and preserve this emotional contact. Yet he remains curiously uncomfortable, and must keep looking back to see whether what he has initiated is still behind him, still intact. Thus he often loses the very thing which he most desires. This figure is deeply paradoxical, as though the element of water – which is in many ways an image of the feminine world of feeling – sits uncomfortably with the masculine and dynamic image of the King. The two are awkward together, and create a strange ambivalence. The King of Cups is a moody and sensitive figure, and often gifted with great depth of feeling and a rare gift at communicating that feeling to affect and influence others. But this is the relationship of performer to audience. He himself never quite relinquishes control. It is for this reason that Dionysos' maenads, the crowd of ecstatic women who follow in the god's train, dismember him, for in a sense he must first be powerless and metaphorically torn to pieces before he can be something other than the wise counsellor to other people's pain. Orpheus himself has no real fulfilment in life, having forfeited his own chance of personal happiness through his mistrust of Hades' word. This in itself tells us a good deal about the King of Cups, for although he may initiate relationship and talk constantly of it, he does not ultimately trust the world of the unconscious, which he cannot see. Thus he is enthroned near the water, but cannot submerge himself in it, for he fears the drowning which letting go to another might entail.

When the King of Cups appears in a spread, it is time for the individual to experience this ambivalent side of himself or herself – the gifted counsellor and healer who can empathize with and help others, yet who cannot quite trust life enough to take its course. It is characteristic that many of those in the helping professions choose such a vocation because they have been wounded through personal relationships, often those with the parents; and thus they form relationships where they remain ultimately in control and cannot be that deeply hurt again. Although this kind of dynamic may contribute a great deal to others, one cheats oneself. If the King of Cups enters the individual's life in the form of a person who embodies these qualities, then this may be taken as an indication that it is time to meet this dimension of oneself.

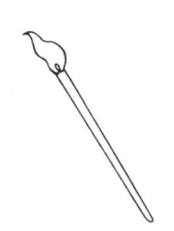

ACE OF WANDS

TWO OF WANDS	 THREE OF WANDS	 FOUR OF WANDS

FIVE OF WANDS	 SIX OF WANDS	 SEVEN OF WANDS

EIGHT OF WANDS	 NINE OF WANDS	 TEN OF WANDS

THE SUIT OF WANDS

The Numbered Cards

The story of Jason and the Argonauts, and their expedition to seek the Golden Fleece, is a characteristic heroic tale, full of adventure and courageous journeying into the unknown. Because the story is really a quest, where the hero must rely on faculties other than will and rational thought, Jason's story may be seen as a portrayal of the creative imagination and its mysterious power to move events and provide solutions from inner levels which elude our conscious understanding. Thus the story of Jason is a specialized adventure which circles around the central motif of the human imagination.

The origin of the Golden Fleece, the magical goal of Jason's quest, was this: Phrixus and Helle, the two children of Athamas the Aeolian, were hated by their stepmother Ino. Their very lives were threatened, and they fled, mounted on a fabulous ram which was the gift of Zeus, king of the gods. This ram was endowed with reason and speech; it had a fleece of gold and could move through the air as well as it could over the earth. In the course of their flight Helle fell into the sea, which was afterward called the Hellespont. Phrixus was luckier, and reached Colchis on the Black Sea. There he sacrificed the ram to his protector Zeus, and offered its fleece to the king of the country, Aeetes, who hung it from a tree and set a dragon who never slept to guard it.

Meanwhile, at Iolkos in Thessaly, reigned King Pelias who had wrenched the throne from his brother Aeson. Aeson's son Jason had been confided to the care of the Centaur Chiron when a baby, to protect him from the wrath of his usurping uncle Pelias. Chiron eventually made known to the child grown to manhood the secret of his origin, and Jason went to his uncle and demanded rule of the kingdom according to his right. Pelias was frightened, for an oracle had warned him of a man wearing one sandal; and this Jason had appeared with only one foot shod, having lost the other sandal while crossing the river. Therefore Pelias promised Jason that he would willingly comply with his demand, but that he had one small request to make: that Jason

THE SUIT OF WANDS

go to Colchis on the Black Sea and bring back the Golden Fleece which properly belonged at Zeus' sanctuary in Iolkos.

So Jason proceeded to build a ship with fifty oars, the *Argo*, in which he had set a bough of the prophetic oak of Zeus from Dodona. He gathered together the most famous heroes, among whom were Castor and Polydeuces (the Warrior Twins), Heracles, Orpheus the Singer, and King Theseus of Athens. Then the hardy adventurers set forth in search of the fabled Golden Fleece. Their voyage was full of incident, and they were forced to struggle against monsters and men as well as against the elements. Finally they reached the kingdom of Aeetes, where the Fleece was kept. Luckily for Jason, King Aeetes' daughter, the sorceress Medea fell in love with him, and helped him to vanquish the dragon which guarded the precious trophy. King Aeetes tried to stop the escaping Argonauts with ferocious soldiers sprung from the teeth of the dragon which Jason had slain; but the heroes managed to sail off in their ship *Argo* with Aeetes in hot pursuit. Medea, who had accompanied Jason, was, however, not averse to stopping her father by the most brutal means, and cut up her brother Absyrtus and scattered the pieces of his body across the water. In grief, Aeetes called his fleet to stop and gather up the dismembered body of the heir, and Jason and his crew now had clear sailing back to Iolkos.

This return voyage, however, proved to be as perilous as the outgoing one, and Jason and his crew once again had to sail through the terrible Clashing Rocks at the north end of the Bosphorus which could crush a ship and which stood between him and safe harbour. At last he reached Iolkos with the Golden Fleece. There he discovered that Pelias had put his father Aeson to death, being certain that Jason would never return from the hazardous voyage. Jason avenged himself on his uncle through Medea, who through her magic spells charmed Pelias' daughters into murdering him. After this Jason reigned as king of Iolkos. But his victory had perhaps gone to his head, for, unsatisfied with one kingship, he sought another – the crown of Corinth – by marrying Creusa, the daughter of Corinth's King Creon. This understandably angered Medea, who avenged herself by murdering not only Creusa but the children she had borne Jason as well.

THE SUIT OF WANDS

As for Jason, some say that he grew weary of life and found the kingship of Iolkos a burden. As an old man, looking forever backward to the day of his glory, he sat dreaming in the shade of the rotting hulk of the *Argo*, and the poop fell on him and crushed him to death.

Ace of Wands

The card of the Ace of Wands portrays a powerfully built, mature man with auburn hair and beard, crowned with gold and robed in imperial purple. He stands regally before a landscape of high snow-capped peaks. Over one shoulder and trailing on to the ground is draped the golden fleece of a ram. In his right hand he holds the globe of the world. In his left he bears a flaming wand.

In the Ace of Wands we meet again Zeus, king of the gods, the initiator and moving power behind the tale of Jason and the Golden Fleece. It is Zeus' sacred Fleece that the hero must obtain, and it is this Fleece which serves as a symbol of the creative vision which spurs us away from the safe, conventional world into unknown paths toward an imagined goal.

Zeus is an ancient and potent god, and one of his oldest representations was the ram-headed deity, the invisible creative power that generated the manifest universe. Thus Zeus embodies within us the invisible creative power of the imagination, which itself cannot be grasped, yet which is responsible for all the strivings and concrete products of our lives. It is not only the artist who uses creative imagination, although in the artist we see its power – and its infuriating autonomy – most clearly. In the Major Arcana card of the Emperor, we met the patriarchal side of Zeus the All-Father. Here, in the Ace of Wands, we meet his volatile spirit, and this Zeus, like Aphrodite, is a force of nature. We all have this power within us. Zeus is the capacity to envision a future potential different from and greater than the concrete reality in which we find ourselves – whether it is a plan for redecorating the sitting room, or a concept for a new business. Many people do not trust this imaginative faculty, believing that it is 'silly' or 'childish', or fearing to take a risk with the new idea because it might fail. But great Zeus is neither silly nor childish, and the Ace of Wands, portraying an initial outpouring of raw creative energy, is a powerful card. The new idea has not yet been formulated, but there is a profound sense of restlessness, and a feeling of life opening up. It is this sense which drives Jason on his quest for the Fleece. He could as easily have simply deposed his uncle Pelias and stayed at home in Iolkos. Thus the Ace of Wands implies the beginning of the great journey into the world of vision and imagination, where concrete limitations are challenged and overcome, and where life is never the same afterward.

On a divinatory level, the Ace of Wands heralds an uprush of creative energy, although this energy has not yet formulated as a goal or project. Restlessness and dissatisfaction with present circumstances are accompanied by a strong feeling that new things are possible. The individual is about to embark on an adventure in pursuit of a vision.

Two of Wands

The card of the Two of Wands portrays the young Jason standing before the Centaur Chiron's cave, poised before he sets out on his journey to reclaim his inheritance. Chiron is dimly visible in the darkness of the cave. Jason, clothed in a scarlet tunic, grips two flaming wands firmly in his hands.

The Two of Wands, like the other Twos of the Minor Arcana, polarizes the raw energy of the Ace, and here that polarization implies the adventurer and his newly conceived goal. The restlessness and unformed power of the Ace has begun to coalesce as a particular vision, although just how that vision might be achieved is not at all clear. Jason does not yet know about the Golden Fleece; but he knows now, because Chiron has told him, that he is a prince and the rightful heir to the throne of Iolkos, and that his father

THE SUIT OF WANDS

Aeson has been deposed and imprisoned by his wicked uncle Pelias. The feeling of potential has here crystallized into something definite, although the real creative adventure of Jason's future – the pursuit of the Golden Fleece – will only emerge once Jason steps forth on the first stage of his journey.

Thus begin all creative ventures: a little at a time. One idea leads to another, and often the first one is not the final one, but merely a prelude. However, the prelude is sufficient to get us moving out of the sanctuary of the cave, because of the feeling that we could have more than we have, or be more than we are. Jason's journey to Iolkos, the place of his rightful inheritance, is fraught with danger, for he has an enemy there who would cheerfully take his life. He cannot predict the outcome, and if he will succeed or fail. But he believes in his vision enough to try, and firmly grips the wands which symbolize the fire of the imagination. Otherwise he – or we – would remain peaceful but forever stifled in the cave, safe but never fulfilling those potentials which are a birthright but which require vision to bring into concrete being.

On a divinatory level, the Two of Wands heralds the formulation of a new aim, idea, goal or creative project. This new idea may not be the final shape of the future, but it is full of potential, and sufficient to lure the individual out of his or her present confines into a new creative venture. Everything here depends upon the courage of the individual to take the new idea up with both hands, and to put faith in that invisible creative power which has generated the vision of the new path.

Three of Wands

The card of the Three of Wands portrays Jason newly arrived at the city of Iolkos. He wears only one sandal, having lost the other in crossing the river, thereby confirming the oracle which has prophesied his advent. He stands triumphantly, holding in his right hand three flaming wands. At his feet kneels the usurper, King Pelias, black-haired and black-bearded, dressed in royal purple, and offering with apparent humility the golden crown which he has unlawfully stolen.

THE SUIT OF WANDS

The Three of Wands, like the other Threes in the Minor Arcana, represents a stage of initial completion. Here it is the apparent completion of the original creative idea. There is a cause for celebration, and it seems everything is going according to plan. Jason has arrived at the place of his inheritance, and lo and behold! he has met with no apparent resistance. Pelias, frightened of the oracle, seems quite willing to abdicate the throne he has stolen. Thus creative work often seems to have an initial ease; the right contacts appear as if by magic, the preliminary sketches look good, and the idea appears to be gathering substance to itself as though it has been prodded by divine intervention.

But there is hard work to come, and often new ideas emerge at this stage – things which we had not at first considered, but which will require delays, alterations of plans, and a lot more effort than had been anticipated. The Three of Wands implies a high point, but there is more to follow. Pelias now tells Jason about the Golden Fleece which lies in Colchis, implying – for his own nasty reasons – that being king of Iolkos means very little without the restoration of Zeus' precious Fleece to the god's sanctuary. It is at this point, after the initial celebration, that many creative potentials collapse, for the stage of initial completion is not a final outcome, and unless the individual is willing to take a further gamble the idea cannot be totally realized. The world is full of unfinished novels sitting in desk drawers, where the first twenty pages started well. The message here is: Enjoy the satisfaction while you can, because you are not finished yet. True creative confidence can only be found if the idea is put to the test and stretches the individual to the utmost.

On a divinatory level, the Three of Wands implies a stage of initial completion of a creative idea or project. Good foundations have been laid, enthusiasm is high, and there is a feeling of satisfaction and optimism about the future potential of the project. . But there is also hard work ahead, and new plans which must be put into action before the full promise can be realized.

THE SUIT OF WANDS

Four of Wands

The card of the Four of Wands portrays Jason celebrating with his shipmates after the building of the great ship Argo which will carry them on their voyage to Colchis to find the Golden Fleece. The ship, decked with scarlet sails bearing the emblem of a golden sunburst, waits on the tide. Around the scarlet-clad figure of Jason stand five of his heroic companions: Heracles (whom we met in the Major Arcana card of Strength), wearing his lion-skin and bearing a flaming wand; Theseus, King of Athens (whom we will meet later in the Minor Arcana card of the King of Wands), crowned with gold and robed in crimson and bearing a flaming wand; Castor and Polydeuces, the Warrior Twins (whom we will meet later in the card of the Knight of Swords), both clad in silver armour and each bearing a flaming wand; and Orpheus the Singer (whom we have met in the card of the King of Cups), clad in a blue robe and holding his lyre.

The Four of Wands is a card of harvest and reward. The challenge of a new creative idea has been met, hard work has been applied, and now the individual can reap the solid reward which has been earned through effort. Like the Three of Wands, this card implies something worth celebrating; but unlike the Three, it has a more solid base, and benefits are already evident. The challenge of capturing the Golden Fleece is a daunting one; how can one man alone sail to the ends of the earth, and in what? Jason has responded to this challenge by gathering around him those friends who can help him to achieve his aims. All these heroes in the myth have different skills, according to their natures. Heracles has strength; Theseus, a fiery adventurer like Jason, has creative vision; the Twins have the cutting edge of the clever mind, and Orpheus has the deep feeling and empathy to disarm any foe. Whether we take these friends as real people whose support we can enlist, or as inner resources upon which we can draw, at this stage of the process of creative work the help is available by which the goal can be reached. With such an heroic crew gathered, and such a splendid ship built, for Jason satisfaction is in order.

On a divinatory level, the Four of Wands augurs a time of reward for

THE SUIT OF WANDS

efforts made. A creative idea has yielded early fruit, and the individual has every right to celebrate the concrete results of his or her efforts. But this is only a stage on the journey, and soon the ship must set sail and face the hardest challenges before the final goal is reached.

Five of Wands

The card of the Five of Wands portrays Jason's battle with the dragon which guards the Golden Fleece. The dragon, huge and covered in greenish scales, belches fire from its mouth while it clutches the precious Fleece in its claws. Jason battles it with two flaming wands. Beside him stands his lover and helper, the sorceress Medea, daughter of King Aeetes of Colchis in whose possession the Fleece has lain. She is beautiful and black-haired, garbed in a flame-coloured gown, and carries three flaming wands.

The Five of Wands represents struggle. Here the creative vision has collided with earthly reality in the form of the dragon which in myth has always represented the primitive powers of the earth which resist change. The problem of accommodating limitations of practical life – and the limitations of one's own regressive inertia – is the greatest challenge to any individual wishing to express the power of his or her creative imagination in actual life. Whether this dragon-fight takes the form of money troubles (shortage of funds, lack of cash flow), or the problem of insufficient skills (where the individual must do further study or training to master a craft), or the difficulty of a protesting body (through fatigue or illness, where we have driven ourselves too hard while in the impatient grip of the vision), or the dilemma of adjusting the vision to the prevailing market (which is inevitably too conservative, cautious or unappreciative) – this card symbolizes trouble on the concrete level. These concrete troubles often coincide with, are caused by or themselves cause a fear of failure and a deep apathy which in themselves are also part of the image of the dragon. But the dragon must be fought or Jason cannot have the Fleece, and the obstacles which arise in the course of creative work – inner or outer – cannot be avoided. The imagination will inevitably collide with the resistance of reality, and somehow the two must be accommodated.

The figure of Medea, the sorceress, is necessary to Jason. Without her, his own vision and courage would be insufficient. She knows how to find the dragon's lair, and how to overcome it. In some ways she is a close cousin of the Major Arcana card of the High Priestess – the mysterious feminine power of the intuition and the instincts, which can be relied upon in such a crisis. Thus the struggle embodied in the Five of Wands requires more than persistance and loyalty to a vision; it also requires a 'gut' sense of timing and a feeling of how the laws of the material world operate.

On a divinatory level, the Five of Wands augurs a time of struggle where the individual must battle with the dragon of material reality to achieve the goal. Mundane matters may begin to go wrong, and more attention must be paid to the demands and limits of concrete reality; or the individual falls into the grip of a depressive or apathetic mood. Compromises must be made while still retaining the integrity of the original vision.

Six of Wands

The card of the Six of Wands portrays Jason victorious after his battle with the dragon. The hero holds the Golden Fleece aloft in triumph. Behind him, six of his hero-companions stand cheering, each bearing a flaming wand.

The Six of Wands represents an experience of triumph, recognition by others, and public acclaim. The battle with the dragon has been fought, and Jason has earned his reward; the Fleece is in his hands, and his crew raise their wands high to honour and acknowledge him. This card represents a heady moment for the individual who has been striving to express some new idea or creative vision to others, for it is the moment when we are given validation by the collective for our efforts. The creative venture has been given the stamp of approval not just by our loved ones, but by the world 'out there', which in the Five appeared initially as the terrible earth-dragon which seemed to thwart all efforts.

The rather intoxicating stage reflected by the Six of Wands can take many forms, according to the height of the goal and the aspirations of the individual. The athlete who has trained and prepared for many weary months or even years knows it when the match is won; the individual aiming for promotion knows it when the new position is at last offered. The writer knows it when the book is published and acclaimed, and the student knows it when the qualification has at last been achieved. Great or small, the goal is here reached and acknowledged by others. Thus the Six of Wands is one of the most satisfying of the cards of the Minor Arcana on an individual level, for it means the public validation of a creative vision which began amidst anxiety and uncertainty.

But even the Six of Wands must give way to the next card, for Jason has not yet brought the Fleece back to Iolkos. Public recognition brings its own dilemmas with it, although it represents a peak in creative life, for the imagination cannot stay still, and further challenges – particularly the envy and competitiveness of others – may arise out of the moment of triumph.

On a divinatory level, the Six of Wands augurs public acclaim or acknowledgement of some kind. This might take the form of a promotion, a qualification, or the recognition of some piece of creative work.

Seven of Wands

The card of the Seven of Wands portrays Jason's battle with King Aeetes of Colchis, which he must win in order to bring the Fleece back to Iolkos. Jason, holding two flaming wands, struggles with the king, who is dressed in a flame-coloured robe and holds a flaming wand. Two of Jason's hero-companions – Heracles and Theseus – battle

THE SUIT OF WANDS

with two of the king's armoured warriors that have sprung from the dragon's teeth. The two heroes and the two Colchian warriors all bear flaming wands.

The Seven of Wands, like the Five, portrays a struggle, but here it is an evenly matched contest of men against men, rather than the creative hero pitted against the alien power of the earth-dragon. The creative vision of the Fleece, won in triumph from the dragon's claws, here leads to what we might call stiff competition, for Aeetes also wants the Fleece and is prepared to fight for it. Thus the recognition which came with the Six here provokes the inevitable response: Somebody else wants what we have worked so hard to achieve, and we are plunged into a contest which challenges us to try even harder. The message is that we cannot rest on our laurels, or someone will come along and steal them. This problem of envy and competition is a fact of creative life, and one which any individual working in this sphere of life must accept. The imagination not only conjures vision in one person, but also stimulates the vision of others as well. Competition is the inevitable companion of creative success and it is often fear of it which keeps many people from trying in the first place.

The challenge of the Seven of Wands is really a test of one's faith in oneself. How hard are we willing to fight for the thing which has been achieved? This onslaught from 'outside' is a stimulus to individuality and also to the imagination itself, which then must create new and better forms. In many respects King Aeetes is as entitled to the Fleece as Jason, for he had it first; and such is the amorality of the market-place, where it is useless to sit down and cry, 'But I had the idea first!' We must simply fight to make the idea work, and make it better, for no one will console the loser because once upon a time he had a good idea.

On a divinatory level, the Seven of Wands augurs a struggle with other people's creative ideas – stiff competition. The individual is challenged to improve upon and develop his or her project in the face of an envious and competitive world and needs to learn to value his or her ambition and competitive instinct.

Eight of Wands

The card of the Eight of Wands portrays Jason's voyage away from Colchis after his safe escape from the angry King Aeetes. We see the ship Argo in full sail, with eight flaming wands lined up upon its deck, streaming fire into the wind. Following the ship's smooth wake, dolphins play among the waves.

The Eight of Wands represents a release of creative energy after the anxieties and struggles of the Seven have been overcome. Conflict stimulates the imagination, and if we have been able to face it and see it through, there is often a period of smooth sailing, where our plans proceed toward the goal at a rapid rate and there is a feeling of buoyancy and confidence. This unlocking of energy only arises out of tensions being released, as though the confidence is gained only through triumphing over obstacles.

The experience of release of new creative energy can be seen in many competitive sports, where after a patch of difficulty there is a sudden burst and the individual or team leaps toward the goal. It is also an experience common to the painter, the writer, the actor and the musician – any creative artist who has broken through a block and is on the 'home stretch'. The exhilaration of this state does not simply arise out of nothing; it must be paid for by meeting the challenge of competition and self-doubt, out of which we rise with renewed energy. This tells us something about why we need conflict in our lives in order to create, and why so many artists seem to court quarrels and competition with others. There is a mysterious relationship between the workings of the creative imagination and the presence of healthy conflict in our lives. Myth also tells us about this relationship, for the god Zeus, who presides over the story of Jason, exists in a state of constant tension and struggle with his wife Hera. She, embodying the laws of marriage and domestic life, perpetually restricts him and in turn challenges him to create. Thus we too need restriction and challenge in order to enjoy the exciting flow of energy which the Eight of Wands portrays through the image of Jason and his crew sailing for home.

THE SUIT OF WANDS

On a divinatory level, the Eight of Wands heralds a period of action after delay or struggle. Travel is sometimes implied, or a clear stretch of fruitful creative activity, where the imagination flows unchecked after anxieties and tensions have been overcome or resolved.

Nine of Wands

The card of the Nine of Wands portrays the final struggle of Jason and his Argonauts before the goal is reached: the passage through the Clashing Rocks. In the distance the city of Iolkos can be seen, with nine flaming wands beckoning on the shore. Around the city the sea is calm. The ship Argo passes with tattered sails between the threatening rocks, not yet safely out the other side. Around the ship a storm rages, and the sea is turbulent.

The Nine of Wands is the card of strength in reserve. It portrays the tremendous power of the creative imagination, for just when we feel we cannot fight one more fight or confront one more difficulty, somehow in the midst of this stress the ideas and the energy become available to take on this final challenge before the goal. The tattered sails of the *Argo* reflect the state of exhaustion of Jason and his crew, for they have passed through many tests and difficulties and are almost home with the Golden Fleece. It is inevitably just at this moment that a final challenge so often arises with our creative ideas and projects. At such a moment one feels one simply cannot go on; the energy is all used up, the strength has gone, and it has all been for nothing.

But there is something mysterious and quite awesome within us which can rise to the challenge at such times, and then we are faced with the most disturbing and miraculous aspect of what we call the creative spirit in human beings. Although we cannot control it or bend it to our will – any more than an ancient Greek could have demanded that Zeus obey human dictates – it is available to help us when we are at our lowest ebb. Then the imagination brings forth a sudden injection of new life, new hope, and new ideas. If we are willing to try once more, the energy is available, and the final goal can be reached.

THE SUIT OF WANDS

On a divinatory level, the Nine of Wands heralds a time when, at the point of exhaustion, a final challenge arises to prevent us reaching our goal; and where, somehow, mysteriously, we can find the strength in reserve to meet the challenge. This strength is only available when we have used up every other possibility, and it seems to be invoked by both our need and our willingness, despite exhaustion, to try one more time.

Ten of Wands

The card of the Ten of Wands portrays Jason sitting wearily before the beached wreck of the Argo. He has returned triumphant to Iolkos, and we see him robed in kingly scarlet robes and wearing a golden crown. The Golden Fleece lies at his feet. He is bowed down by the heavy weight of the ten flaming wands which lie across his back and shoulders.

The Ten of Wands portrays a state of oppression. Jason has achieved everything he has set out to do; yet, at the end of the tale, he is a sad figure, overburdened and weighed down with cares, while the once glorious ship *Argo*, carrier of heroes, lies mouldering. It is at first difficult to understand why this fiery tale of vision and heroic exploits should culminate in an image which is heavy and careworn. But this last numbered card of the Suit of Wands tells something important about the creative imagination: It can no longer function when it has become trapped under the weight of worldly responsibilities.

This hard lesson happens to many people who set out to start a business, or aim for creative success. As time goes on and the business gets larger and more solid, the excitement and enthusiasm that existed at first seem to vanish. Jason has, in the process of achieving his goal and taking up his kingship, neglected to value those unpredictable elements, such as Medea personifies, and has thus 'sold out', forgetting the daring and unconventionality that pushed him into adventure in the first place. The volatile power of the imagination resists being captured in heavy and structured forms. Boredom and depression often accompany the completion of a creative work, for while the tension of the struggle to earth creative ideas generates more ideas, the final concretization of them means the imagination can no longer freely express itself.

Thus the imagination must have fresh pastures, and the individual who like Jason clings too tightly to the form he or she has built may find a sense of oppression and exhaustion without apparent reason. Then it may be time to relinquish some of the safety and security so that the imagination can awaken again with a new idea, a new goal and a new gamble.

On a divinatory level, the Ten of Wands implies that the individual is overburdened and oppressed by having taken on more than he or she can deal with. The imagination has been stifled by too many worldly concerns, and some of the youthful daring and willingness to take risks have been lost. Certain things may need to be relinquished so that the creative process can be refreshed and a new cycle may begin.

THE SUIT OF WANDS

The Court Cards

Page of Wands

The card of the Page of Wands portrays a boy of around twelve years of age, with curling auburn hair and wearing a pale orange tunic. He rides on the back of a golden-fleeced ram which flies over the yellow and green fields and streams, holding a flaming wand whose fire streams out into the wind behind him. Ahead of him is a rising sun which casts a vivid orange glow over the landscape.

Here, in the card of the Page of Wands, we meet the element of fire in its most delicate and fragile beginnings – the first stirrings of creative inspiration which usually manifest as a kind of restlessness and unease with existing conditions. This is embodied in the mythic figure of Phrixus, whom we briefly met in the story of Jason and the Golden Fleece which illustrates the numbered cards of the Suit of Wands. Phrixus really begins this tale, although he is not one of the heroes who partake in it, nor is he the god who presides over it; for it is he who takes the Fleece out of danger and over land and sea to the distant kingdom of Colchis.

Phrixus was the son of King Athamas. This Athamas was married to a phantom-woman called Nephele on the command of Zeus, and she

THE SUIT OF WANDS

bore him both the boy Phrixus and a girl called Helle. But the phantom-woman eventually vanished, and Athamas married a mortal woman, Ino, who was jealous both of her predecessor and of the children by this supernatural marriage. Ino persuaded the women of the countryside to parch the seed-corn secretly so that the harvest would fail, and then claimed that the Delphic Oracle demanded the sacrifice of Phrixus to the god Zeus to lift the 'curse'. Thus she intended to make way for a child of her own to be the king's heir.

But Zeus resented having his name used for such vindictive conniving, and sent a winged golden ram to rescue Phrixus. The boy mounted the ram and pulled his sister up behind him, and the ram flew eastwards, making for the land of Colchis. Helle lost her hold, and fell into the sea; but Phrixus reached Colchis and sacrificed the ram to Zeus the Deliverer. Thus he is a kind of messenger or stage-setter who opens the action before the better-known heroes enter the stage.

Phrixus, the Page of Wands, is an image of that fragile beginning of the creative imagination which is often at odds with more realistic people and the demands and responsibilities of the mundane world. The danger in which the boy finds himself is not uncharacteristic of the Page of Wands, for this figure, although promising a future potential that has not yet emerged, often manifests first as irritability and restlessness which often provokes others and causes problems in one's personal life and work. Yet Phrixus is innocent, and because of his innocence Zeus favours him and makes him the recipient of a great gift. The Page of Wands marks the bare beginnings of the emergence of a new creative idea, but like all the Pages of the Minor Arcana he needs care, protection and nurturing lest his gentle small fire be quenched by the jealousy or anger of others, or by one's own negativity and narrowness. Zeus, king of the gods and embodiment of the fiery creative spirit, is the only one to give Phrixus his true value, and we must have some contact with this archetypal principle within ourselves before we can value these delicate beginnings of imaginative expression.

Phrixus opens the tale, but he does not remain in it, and vanishes before the greater flamboyance and power of the hero Jason. This too reflects something about the Page of Wands. The early young ideas which are reflected by this card are often childlike (or childish), and do not represent the final form which ends in a major creative effort. Often the early concept vanishes, to be replaced by something better and stronger. But the initial beginning ushers a process into activity, and without this fragile stirring nothing at all would ever be developed in the realm of new creative ideas. And ultimately it is not the character of Phrixus which comes down to us in myth – he is too young and unformed to really possess a character – but his role as messenger and initial custodian of the Golden Fleece which belongs to Zeus and which is the emblem of the god's great creative power. Thus the Page of Wands may not indicate a new project or idea which is guaranteed to succeed, and his stirrings may be easily dismissed as 'silly' or 'fantastic'. He serves as a pointer to the power of the imagination, and tells us that there is a lot more where the first idea came from.

When the Page of Wands appears in a spread, it is time for the individual to discover some new stirring of creative potential within himself or herself. This may often manifest as restlessness at work, a vague feeling of dissatisfaction not yet strong enough to motivate a change, and a hint or glimpse that one might be able to expand one's life in some way. The initial fantasies which accompany such restlessness do not have the uprushing power of the Ace of Wands, and may ultimately turn out to be impractical or impossible. Yet it is important to take them seriously, for they are the harbingers of a stronger source of inspiration, and need to be nurtured rather than stamped upon as though such restlessness were merely a 'bad phase' rather than a herald.

Knight of Wands

The card of the Knight of Wands portrays an exuberant, flamboyant young man, wearing a scarlet tunic and gold armour and helmet. He rides on a winged horse. A quiver of arrows is slung over his shoulder, and in his hand he holds a flaming wand. The white horse is flying upward through the air, while below, on the ochre-coloured

THE SUIT OF WANDS

earth, lies a dead monster which has been slain by the young man's arrow. This beast has the head of a lion, the body of a goat and a serpent's tail.

Here, in the card of the Knight of Wands, we meet the volatile, changeable, effervescent dimension of the element of fire, which is always in motion and perpetually seeking new challenges. This is embodied in the mythic figure of the hero Bellerophon, who mastered the wild winged horse Pegasus and killed the monstrous Chimaera, and then was undone by his own arrogance as he tried to fly to Olympus, the abode of the gods.

Bellerophon had to leave his native Corinth under a cloud, for having killed a rival and then his own brother. These deeds were not committed through malice, but through too high spirits, and Bellerophon then sought sanctuary with King Proetus of Tiryns. But Proetus' wife fell in love with the dashing and rather ambiguous young man, and although Bellerophon refused her advances, King Proetus believed she had been seduced and resolved to destroy the hero. He was thus sent on an apparently fatal mission – the destruction of the Chimaera, a fire-breathing she-monster. But the young man found luck in the form of a seer, who advised him to catch and tame the winged horse Pegasus. Bellerophon found the horse and threw over its head a golden bridle which Athene had given him. He then overcame the Chimaera by flying above her on Pegasus' back, riddling her with arrows, and then thrusting between her jaws a lump of lead which he had fixed to the point of his spear. The Chimaera's fiery breath melted the lead, which trickled down her throat and killed her.

Bellerophon, far from displaying the appropriate modesty about his heroic deed, became arrogant and boastful. At the height of his fortune, he presumptuously tried to fly to Olympus as though he were immortal. Zeus, infuriated, sent a gadfly which stung Pegasus under the tail, making the horse rear and fling Bellerophon ingloriously to earth.

Bellerophon, the Knight of Wands, is an image of the craving for new and ever more glorious adventures. This highly ambivalent figure is

THE SUIT OF WANDS

both immensely creative and divorced from reality, for although he is the first to 'smell' new things in the wind and also the first to take up a challenge, however difficult, he is also our propensity for inflation and a kind of childlike assumption that good luck always ought to be handed out by life no matter what we are or what we do. The Knight of Wands is a charmer – women tend to love him, as does the wife of King Proetus in the myth – but he is unreliable, since no woman can hold him when a new adventure beckons. He is intuitive and imaginative, and in modern terms we might also call him 'trendy', for he is the first to take up a new idea, a new fashion, a new lifestyle long before the plodding remainder of humanity discovers that the new thing might be worthwhile. The Knight of Wands is no follower, although he is no leader either, for he is too self-centred and easily bored to take up the responsibility of directing others. Like Don Quixote in Cervantes' great tale, he tilts at windmills, often taking up a cause or challenge which may not really be relevant but about which he is prepared to make a considerable amount of noise just because it seems exciting and will gain him attention as well as keeping him occupied for a time. The Knight of Wands is a likeable figure, even lovable, and we tend to forgive him a lot because of his natural high spirits, attractiveness, naivete, and well-meaning intent. But the road to hell, as they say, is paved with good intentions, and not all of this figure's intentions are put into concrete form. He is most creative spinning new ideas which can be sifted, considered, and processed through a more realistic lens, either by oneself or someone else who is more in touch with the earth than this volatile, fiery Knight. Then his strengths can be enjoyed while his weaknesses are made less harmful by cool consideration of the facts.

When the Knight of Wands appears in a spread, it is time for the individual to develop the volatile, exuberant and adventurous qualities embodied in the figure of Bellerophon. Often on a divinatory level the Knight of Wands manifests as a change of residence, because the individual suddenly feels too cramped by his or her environment and seeks broader and greener pastures. Sometimes the Knight of Wands will enter one's life in the form of a charming, exciting and rather unreliable young man, full of new ideas, who inspires but who must be taken with the proverbial grain of salt lest he lead one into a bad fall. But if such an individual enters one's sphere, it should be seen as an augury that these qualities are trying to emerge from within oneself.

Queen of Wands

The card of the Queen of Wands portrays a beautiful, radiant woman with rich auburn hair, dressed in a saffron-coloured robe and wearing a golden crown. She is seated on a golden throne whose arms are carved with lions' heads, and at her feet on a golden chain lies a sleeping lioness. In her hand is a flaming wand. Around her stretches a landscape of rich green and gold fields under a vivid blue sky.

Here, in the card of the Queen of Wands, we meet the stable, vivifying, loyal dimension of the element of fire which warms and heartens as it inspires. This is embodied in the mythic figure of Queen Penelope, the wife of the famous wandering hero Odysseus of Ithaca. At her birth, Penelope had been flung into the sea at her father Icarius' order; for he had hoped for a male child. But a flock of purple-striped ducks buoyed her up, fed her, and towed her ashore. Impressed by this prodigy, Icarius relented, aware that his young daughter must possess some special destiny.

When her husband Odysseus embarked for the Trojan War along with all the other Greek princes, Penelope was left to run the island kingdom with only her young son Telemachus to help her. Presuming Odysseus' death, no less than one hundred and twelve insolent young princes of the islands around Ithaca began to court Penelope, each hoping to marry her and take the throne; and they had agreed amongst themselves to murder Telemachus. When they first asked Penelope to decide between them, she held faith with her intuition and her heart about her husband's safety, and declared that he must certainly be alive. Later, hard-pressed, she promised a decision as soon as she completed the shroud which she must weave against the death of old Laertes, her

THE SUIT OF WANDS

father-in-law. But she took three years over the task, weaving by day and unravelling the work by night, until at last the suitors detected the ruse. All this time they were disporting themselves in Odysseus' palace, consuming his food and wine and seducing his maidservants.

Odysseus meanwhile arrived home after ten years of wandering, disguised as a beggar because he had been informed of the activities at his palace. When Penelope sent for the 'beggar' she did not at first recognize him, but eventually he revealed himself, destroyed the insolent suitors, and was happily reunited with his wife. Some deny, however, that Penelope remained faithful to Odysseus during his long absence, since she was a lady of spirit and inventiveness. They accuse her of bearing the god Pan to Hermes the Messenger, which may or may not be true.

Penelope, the Queen of Wands, is an image of the loyalty of the heart and the strength of the creative imagination to sustain the heart's chosen goals. She is in one sense a picture of the faithful wife; but her faithfulness is not necessarily a literal one, and some versions of the myth question this technical sexual loyalty. Penelope's loyalty springs from a much deeper level. All through the years of her husband's absence she has no way of knowing whether he is dead or alive, and at times it would obviously be more convenient to choose another husband and get on with her life. Yet she knows intuitively that Odysseus will return, and it is this quality of faith and a loyalty which springs not from enforced morality but from a deep inner conviction that in the end everything will turn out right, that makes Penelope so suitable a figure to illustrate the Queen of Wands. This figure is industrious, creative, versatile, strong-willed and talented, as we might expect from any of the representatives of the Suit of Wands. But she is also self-contained and stable, for her fire is banked and becomes the warmth of the hearth-fire, a centre to which many are attracted – like the hundred and twelve suitors who are drawn not only to the kingdom, but to the woman. The Queen of Wands does not go chasing after rainbows or trying to fly to Olympus – pastimes more typical of the Knight. She holds her great strength and energy within, and devotes

THE SUIT OF WANDS

them to those few things to which she has given her heart. In some ways Penelope, the Queen of Wands, is an ancient image of that 'superwoman' figure toward which so many modern women aspire: the woman who is capable of loyalty and love in relationship, yet who also has the strength, ingenuity, creativity and tireless energy to rule her own world in her own right and to need no strong shoulder to lean on or socially acceptable label of 'wife' to make her a worthwhile and self-confident individual.

When the Queen of Wands appears in a spread, it is time for the individual to begin to develop these qualities of warmth, constancy, loyalty and creative sustaining of a vision which Penelope so aptly symbolizes. The Queen of Wands may enter one's life as such an imaginative and magnetic woman, full of warmth and life. But if such a person enters one's sphere it is not by chance, but rather an augury that the individual is about to meet these attributes within.

King of Wands

The card of the King of Wands portrays a handsome, fiery man with curling chestnut hair and beard. He is clad in a rich crimson robe and a golden crown, and is seated on a golden throne whose arms are carved with golden rams' heads. In his hand he holds a flaming wand. Around him are vivid green fields in which a ram can be seen poised with its head held high. Behind him rise the white pillars and porticoes of a beautiful city crowned with an acropolis.

Here, in the card of the King of Wands, we meet the active, dynamic, lordly dimension of the element of fire, which symbolizes the creative imagination. This is embodied in the mythic figure of King Theseus of Athens, whom we met briefly in the numbered cards of the Suit of Wands as one of the companions of Jason on his adventure to capture the Golden Fleece. King Theseus personifies all the exciting, outgoing, impulsive, bad-tempered and

THE SUIT OF WANDS

tremendously infectious spirit of fiery energy. His mother Aethra was loved both by the god Poseidon and King Aegeus of Athens. Theseus was jointly fathered by them but did not know of his origins until he was sixteen. He then set out on many dangerous adventures to claim his place as Aegeus' heir. He offered himself as one of the tribute of youths and maidens to be sent to Crete to be fed to the terrible Minotaur, enchanted King Minos' daughter Ariadne into helping him destroy the monster, and returned to Athens in triumph, passing through not only violent combat with the monster but also fire, earthquake, riot, and terrible seas. When he became King of Athens in Aegeus' place he was full of new and brilliant ideas of how to unite the constantly warring Greek city-states, and through a combination of charm, good salesmanship, physical prowess, a flair for the dramatic and a brilliant mind, managed to persuade these independent and haughty lords to pull together under one yoke over which he presided as High King.

The adventures of Theseus in love were as chequered and turbulent as his feats of arms. A ceaseless pursuer of women, he eventually chose as his queen the Amazon Hippolyta, a warrior-woman who was hardly content to live in domestic tranquillity but insisted on fighting beside him in all his battles. After her death he roved the seas as a pirate, returning periodically to Athens but always pursuing the next dream, the next conquest. Eventually he married Phaedra, a Cretan princess, who unfortunately fell in love with her stepson Hippolytus, Theseus' child by the Amazon. This tangle resulted in Phaedra's suicide and Hippolytus' death, after which Theseus steadily deteriorated until he threw himself off a high rock into the sea.

Theseus, the King of Wands, is an image of the fiery enthusiasm which makes an individual, man or woman, a true leader. This fiery spirit is not merely impulse and restlessness and fresh ideas – these things we have found in the Knight of Wands – but also contains an innate nobility and strength. Theseus is not just a brash young man. He is a strategist and a shaper of world events, for he possesses not only vision but the steady power to manifest his vision and the warm and infectious personality which can convince others of its validity. He is

THE SUIT OF WANDS

intolerant of limitation, impatient and certain that he is right, and he is unquestionably a bad loser. King Theseus of the myth is also the epitome of the male chauvinist, and this quality is not necessarily limited to men alone, but can equally be found in many women. It is a spirit of exalting the masculine pursuits of adventure, conflict, and conquest, while undervaluing the quieter and more 'ordinary' dimensions of emotional and material life – which seem demeaning, boring and therefore not worth wasted time and effort. King Theseus is irresistible because he is so much larger than life, and this quality in human nature, which tends to mythologize itself as well as selling a grand vision to others, is likewise irresistible and dynamic. Those individuals in whom the spirit of the King of Wands expresses strongly are never content to be 'mere' mortals. There must be a cause to espouse, a dragon to slay, a challenge to be met, an imperfection in the world which must be corrected. For the individual who has no inner acquaintance with the spirit of the King of Wands, such people are at best hypnotic and fascinating and at worst pushy, irritating, power-driven and dangerous. Yet without this quality there is no spirit of striving and no capability of improving the lot of oneself or others, for there is no vision and no confidence to turn the vision into reality. The King of Wands may be warm and exciting, but he is unquestionably selfish, and his essential selfishness seems to many to be reprehensible and 'bad'. Yet King Theseus is the embodiment of the true hero, for his vision is always that humanity might be more than it is.

When the King of Wands appears in a spread, it is time for the individual to encounter that dimension of the personality which initiates new ideas and sells them to others, thereby generating change in one's own life and in the immediate environment. It is the spirit of leadership, the belief that one has a better idea which is worth promulgating and working to make manifest. This dimension of life may appear in the form of a fiery, impulsive individual entering one's sphere, someone who infects others with the power of his ideas. But if such a person enters one's life it is not by chance, but is rather an augury of one's own need for development.

	ACE OF SWORDS	

TWO OF SWORDS	 THREE OF SWORDS	 FOUR OF SWORDS

FIVE OF SWORDS	 SIX OF SWORDS	 SEVEN OF SWORDS

EIGHT OF SWORDS	 NINE OF SWORDS	 TEN OF SWORDS

THE SUIT OF SWORDS

The Numbered Cards

The story of Orestes and the curse of the House of Atreus is a dark tale, full of conflict and bloodshed, and one of the most powerful of Greek myths. At its core lies a conflict of two great opposing principles – mother-right and father-right – and it is this collision of principles which makes the tale appropriate for illustrating the quarrelsome, turbulent yet ultimately immensely creative Suit of Swords. For this Suit deals with the human mind in its most potent form: the capacity to create good or evil fate according to the strength of one's beliefs, convictions and principles.

The entire tale of the curse of the House of Atreus is long and convoluted, and we will deal here primarily with its final chapter. But, in short, it begins with the crime of King Tantalos of Lydia, who grew so arrogant that in his madness he mocked the gods. He cut his little son into pieces and served these, cooked, at a banquet to which he had invited the Olympians, in order to test their wisdom. For this act of savagery and arrogance the gods cursed Tantalos' line. Thus the curse of the House of Atreus commences with the misuse of the mind: man's double-edged gift, which raises him above the beasts yet also gives him the power to destroy wantonly.

We begin our exploration of the Suit of Swords with Orestes, the young prince of Argos, who found that the family curse passed on to him in the form of a terrible choice. Orestes was the son of King Agamemnon and Queen Clytemnestra of Argos, and the curse had passed down through Agamemnon's father and grandfather. When the great war began between the Greeks and Trojans (the beginning of which we glimpsed in the story of Paris in the Major Arcana card of the Lovers), Agamemnon was one of the Greek warlords who was elected to lead the armies by sea to Troy. He managed through his arrogance to offend the goddess Hecate (Artemis), by boasting in one of her sacred groves, and Hecate in anger sent a terrible storm which pinned the Greek fleet in harbour. The goddess' oracle informed Agamemnon that he would have to make a dreadful reparation to the goddess before she

THE SUIT OF SWORDS

would lift the storm: He was required to sacrifice his own daughter Iphigenia on the goddess' altar at Aulis, or else to forego the potential glory of leading the Greek armies to Troy. For Agamemnon, glory was far more important than a daughter – after all, he had another, called Electra, and daughters were less valuable than sons – and so he deceived his wife Clytemnestra by announcing that Iphigenia would be married at Aulis. The girl was duly sent from her home at Argos to the war camp at Aulis, and was there slaughtered. By the time Clytemnestra discovered the truth, Agamemnon had already sailed to Troy.

The Greek armies were successful and Troy was sacked, and Agamemnon returned home a hero. But during his absence Clytemnestra plotted revenge for the death of their daughter. She took a lover, Aegisthus, and together these two planned Agamemnon's murder. When he arrived home, surrounded by cheering troops, she greeted him sweetly and led him to his bath; and there she and her lover cut him to pieces. To prevent any interference with this act, she sent her son Orestes away to the city of Phocis, so that he would know nothing of the murder and would not try to save or avenge his father.

But the god Apollo appeared before Orestes in Phocis and told him that he must avenge the murder of his father, for this was the sacred obligation of a son. Orestes protested, horrified, because this meant he must become a matricide. Apollo then threatened him with madness and frightful punishments if Orestes refused the god's command. The young prince at last accepted the will of the god with a heavy heart, for to kill his own mother – although right according to Apollo's patriarchal law – meant he would be hounded into madness and death by the Furies, the terrifying goddesses of vengeance, to whom the murder of a mother was the worst of all human crimes according to their matriarchal law. Thus Orestes accepted his fate, and journeyed back to Argos in secret.

When he arrived at the palace only his dog recognized him; but eventually so did his surviving sister Electra, who also burned with a desire to avenge her father's death. Orestes, with the help of his sister, killed first Aegisthus and then his mother. Thus he fulfilled Apollo's will, but immediately the Furies appeared with their snake-locks and

THE SUIT OF SWORDS

leather wings and horrible faces, and drove him mad with terrible nightmares and visions. They hounded him all over Greece, until eventually in despair and exhaustion he sought sanctuary at the shrine of the goddess Athene. Athene took pity on the young prince who was, through no moral fault of his own, caught between two such powerful and destructive forces. She set up a jury of twelve human judges who might assess the case. The jury was split in its vote – six sided with Apollo and asserted that a father was the most important life, and six sided with the Furies and asserted that it was a mother. Athene herself cast the deciding vote in favour of Orestes just as he was at the point of expiring. The goddess then made peace with the Furies by offering them their own shrine and honourable worship, and thus Orestes was freed and the ancient curse of the House of Atreus was lifted at last.

Ace of Swords

The card of the Ace of Swords portrays a severely beautiful woman in full battle armour, wearing a war helmet. She stands in a menacing posture, and holds aloft a double-edged silver sword. Behind her can be seen a vista of snow-clad mountains and a cold grey sky filled with scudding clouds.

In the Ace of Swords we meet once again Athene, goddess of Justice, whom we first encountered in the Major Arcana card of Justice. Although Athene was not the initiator of the curse of the House of Atreus, nonetheless it is she who resolves it when Orestes turns to her in his desperation. Athene's sword is double-edged, for the cutting power of the mind with its uniquely human capacity to formulate ideas and convictions which spur actions and consequences to those actions, can generate both terrible suffering and sublime new resolutions. Thus Athene's sword cuts both ways, for it is passionate and even rigid adherence to a principle which inaugurates the conflict of the tale; and it is the emergence of a new and more viable principle which resolves and ends it.

THE SUIT OF SWORDS

The Ace of Swords, like the Ace of Cups and the Ace of Wands, heralds a burst of raw energy, and here it is the initial eruption of a new world-view. But such a new perception immediately threatens the old order, and so the Ace of Swords, although its energy is powerful and potentially creative, signals the beginning of great conflict. The awakening of mental powers often means an inevitable collision with the beliefs which have previously been part and parcel of one's life. Having a new idea of things is not as simple as it sounds, for we human beings have been known to wage wars and indulge in terrible acts of savagery in the name of a new principle. We have only to look at the French Revolution of 1789 and Russian Revolution of 1917 to understand how very potent is a new idea, and how often it sets alight a great conflict before it is integrated into life. Even on a more personal level, the raw new energy of the mind stirring into life usually precipitates arguments, debates and quarrels, for we must try out the new thing first and assert our mental autonomy before any dialogue or compromise is possible. Thus the Ace of Swords is truly a double-edged card: a herald of tremendous new energy ready to pour out into life, yet also a warning of conflict to come.

On a divinatory level, the Ace of Swords implies that out of conflict some new creative viewpoint will emerge. The mental powers are awakening and this means change in one's life; the old order is threatened, and conflicts are bound to arise. Ultimately a resolution will be possible but there is an inevitability of collision and struggle before such a peace is in sight.

Two of Swords

The card of the Two of Swords portrays Orestes, fair-haired and clothed in a grey tunic, standing as though paralyzed with eyes tightly closed and his hands pressed over his ears. On the left stands his mother, Queen Clytemnestra, golden-haired and golden-crowned, dressed in a pale lilac gown. She holds a sword with its point directly before the young prince, and stares angrily over his head at her husband, King Agamemnon, fair-haired

THE SUIT OF SWORDS

with a blonde beard, dressed in sky-blue tunic and full battle armour. He likewise holds a sword with its point directly before Orestes. Behind them can be seen mountain peaks, and a darkening sky with ominous clouds.

The Two of Swords reflects a state of paralysis, where opposing forces have created a standstill and no movement is possible lest some conflagration be unleashed. Orestes is here shown caught between the opposing forces of his mother and father. In response to this state of tension which demands a choice of some kind, he has elected to see and hear nothing – and his refusal to become conscious of the impending conflict is the only action he can at this point offer. The situation of the Two of Swords thus reflects a tension where an unpleasant reality must be faced; yet the individual is unwilling to upset the status quo, and closes his eyes and ears to the problem. Blinded in this way, Orestes manages not to be unhappy, but he is not happy either, for he cannot move or grow. He is too terrified of upsetting the balance, although this balance is not harmonious and a storm looms behind the tense figures.

The polarization which occurs in all the Twos of the Minor Arcana here formulates as a conflict of opposing principles. But this balance has not arisen from dialogue and interchange; it is tense and full of potential destructiveness. Thus, when a new view of life has begun to stir in us with the Ace of Swords, we tend to see only the extremes, and are caught in a kind of paralysis where we cannot move either forward or back. We are unable to pretend that nothing has happened; but we cannot go ahead either, or trouble will ensue. The emotional tone of the Two of Swords is an uncomfortable state of precariously balanced calm, beneath which there is great tension and anxiety. It is the state of knowing that something must change, but being terrified of doing anything to inaugurate the change, preferring to blind oneself rather than risk the conflict which must, eventually, happen anyway.

On a divinatory level, the Two of Swords implies a state of tense balance where there is a refusal to face some impending situation of

THE SUIT OF SWORDS

conflict. A more creative way of handling this situation might be to try to face what is before one, rather than attempting to preserve the status quo, which will eventually be disrupted anyway.

Three of Swords

The card of the Three of Swords portrays King Agamemnon slaughtered in his bath. The dead body of the king lies slackly in the water. On the left, Aegisthus, black-haired and black-bearded and robed in dark grey, pierces the king's heart with a sword. Another sword stands upright, its point buried in the inert body. On the right stands Clytemnestra, also piercing her husband's heart with a sword. Beyond the marble portico can be seen a black, brooding sky lowering over mountain peaks.

The Three of Swords is a sorrowful card, because the strife or conflict impending in the Two has at last erupted and come out into the open. Thus the theme of initial completion which links all the Threes in the Minor Arcana is here reflected in a painful situation, where some separation or heartbreak has revealed itself. Yet while it is painful, this card, which is undoubtedly a difficult one, represents a release of energy, for at least there is movement from the stagnant and unpleasant tension of the Two. Whatever has happened is in some way necessary, because something is at work which requires such conflict before it can unfold to its eventual creative end. Here Clytemnestra has had her revenge, and this revenge was inevitable from the moment that Agamemnon chose his own glory over the life of his daughter. Something set in motion in the past comes to fruition in the Three of Swords, and the fruit is rarely pleasant. This is the deepest meaning of the curse in Greek myth: not a spell or bad fate cast by some capricious god, but the inevitable working out of the consequences of human choice over time, which sooner or later will result in heartbreak or conflict when the bill comes due.

The sorrowful vision of the Three of Swords thus brings with it a feeling of relief, for the poison has come out, and therefore a chance of future healing becomes possible. Resentments which have remained subterranean because we are frightened of conflict and anger have a way of bursting through at last, but often through the next generation, who are forced to act out the problems which the preceding ones refused to face. Unpleasant though the Three of Swords is, it is nevertheless a creative step from the Two, and an ultimate resolution is now possible.

On a divinatory level, the Three of Swords heralds strife, conflict or separation. This painful state is in some way necessary, and there is a realization that blindness and self-delusion cannot go on. This is like the breaking of an abcess, so that the body can begin to heal.

Four of Swords

The card of the Four of Swords portrays Orestes in exile in Phocis. He sits peacefully on the ground, contemplating four swords which lie in a pattern before him. Behind him can be seen a pale, quiet sky with little puffs of cloud, and a vista of snow-clad peaks.

The Four of Swords reflects a quiet time of withdrawal and contemplation. Here we see Orestes in the place of his banishment. He has not yet received his command from the god Apollo, and so he is at peace, although he is not permitted to go home. The Four of Swords suggests a period of introversion and reflection, of emotional recuperation after the outbreak of conflict in the Three. The poison has been released and there is now an opportunity to reflect upon what has happened. This is a period of preparation before the task of making what changes are necessary in life as a result of the conflict. There is a building up of strength, a marshalling of inner reserves in a situation of stillness and introspection.

We instinctively seek this place of quiet after some major disruptive or painful event has occurred in our lives. The individual who has gone through separation or divorce, or even a bad quarrel, often needs time alone to examine the pattern of what has happened; so too does the

THE SUIT OF SWORDS

person who is bereaved, or thrown out of work, or parted with a friend or loved one. Often we do not recognize the value of this time of quiet, but try to rush out and surround ourselves with people who will make us feel better and help us to forget what has happened. But Orestes' banishment is a forcible one, and in some ways we are forced into introversion by the discovery that all the frenzied rushing about does not cure anything at all. We often feel worse, until we can recognize the need for silence and solitude before going out into life again. Such reflection can reveal the meaning underlying the separation or conflict, because any difficulty reflected by the Suit of Swords will inevitably point backward to some stage where a new view of life has begun to emerge and is upsetting all our pre-existing patterns of living.

On a divinatory level, the Four of Swords heralds a time of quiet recuperation and introversion, where the individual can build up strength in preparation for further efforts. If this card appears in a spread, it is perhaps wise to accept solitude or withdrawal, and not seek to fill the time with activities; for some stillness is needed to marshal one's thoughts and order one's life.

Five of Swords

The card of the Five of Swords portrays Orestes, seated on the ground, facing the god Apollo, who has appeared to tell him of his fate and his obligation – to avenge his father's death. Apollo stands on the right, and points sternly at the five swords which he holds in his right hand. In the distance, dark clouds can be seen hovering over the mountain peaks.

The Five of Swords represents acceptance of limitations, boundaries and the confines of destiny. Here Orestes must come to terms with his blighted family inheritance, and accept the task which has been imposed upon him. That his allotment is unfair is not the point; he must face what is before him without complaining, whining or dodging, for it is through this acceptance of his own destiny that he can progress and earn his right to manhood and eventual kingship. It is also important that Orestes accept the god's law not out of fear alone – although Apollo's threats are frightening enough – but because he himself recognizes its necessity. He is a man, and therefore for him Apollo's patriarchal law is his law. Had he been a daughter, such a lot would not have fallen upon him. But the implication here is that, when faced with such a profound choice, Orestes must in the end offer his loyalty to that masculine principle which lies at the root of his own sexual identity, regardless of the consequences.

Limitations and their necessary acceptance, as portrayed by the Five of Swords, often require us to swallow false pride as well as fear. Sometimes the individual has overstepped his or her boundaries, and has tried to achieve something which is too inflated. Recognition of one's limits requires consciousness and a clear, unbiased mind. One knows what one is, and therefore what one can and must do; this is acceptance of inner law. Although this can be distressing, or even depressing, or apparently belittling, nevertheless it is a stage which is necessary if the individual wishes to make effective the principles in which he or she believes. Without this acceptance of one's own lot, nothing can be accomplished.

On a divinatory level, the Five of Swords augurs the necessity of facing one's own limits, and recognizing that life needs to be lived within the confines of one's capabilities. Often there is a situation where the individual has taken on too much, and must swallow pride and back off, facing honestly what is possible before moving forward.

Six of Swords

The card of the Six of Swords portrays Orestes standing in a dignified posture in a shallow boat. He is wrapped in a pale mauve cloak, and stares across the water toward the city of Argos which can be seen in the distance. Six swords stand upright, their points

THE SUIT OF SWORDS

embedded in the hull of the boat. In the foreground the waters are turbulent, and storm-clouds can be seen in the sky. But as Orestes approaches his city, the water can be seen to be calmer, and the sky above the city is clear.

The Six of Swords portrays a situation of moving away from turbulent, difficult feelings toward a calmer and more serene state. Some consciousness has been gained, and some peace, from the acceptance of one's limits in the Five; and now there is a calmer, if still melancholy, path ahead. The Six of Swords is not a 'happy' card, but it suggests a harmony which springs from coming to terms with one's limits and tasks. Thus the young prince, although moving toward a terrible deed, is nevertheless at peace within himself, and leaves behind him the anxious, distressing and fraught state suggested by the choppy waters behind him.

The serene state suggested by the Six of Swords is not really pleasurable like the nostalgia of the Six of Cups; it does not spring from a tranquil heart, but rather from a tranquil mind. Insight and understanding mean everything here, for the serenity and smooth passage of the Six of Swords depend upon one's seeing and comprehending the way in which the pattern of one's life works. It is this need for seeing and understanding which causes many people to study subjects like the Tarot and astrology, as well as psychology and the workings of the human mind, during times of difficulty; for understanding makes an enormous difference when we are beset by problems, and seeing how we have architected our own fates can often release the anxiety and promote a calm acceptance which allows us to move into the future. The gifts which such symbolic maps as the Tarot or the horoscope offer are beyond price, although a map cannot make choices for us, or change an external situation from bad into good. But knowledge of why we are on a particular road, and how we got there, and what it might mean, can sometimes work magic; and thus the sea changes toward a calm and peaceful passage.

On a divinatory level, the Six of Swords suggests a time when the mind's capacity for understanding helps to ease a difficult and anxiety-provoking time into a more peaceful passage. Insight smooths the storm-clouds, and one can retain one's dignity and self-respect.

Seven of Swords

The card of the Seven of Swords portrays Orestes, shrouded and hooded in his cloak, stealthily creeping into the palace at Argos. In his arms he carries seven swords. The street is dark, and the palace doorway is a black and unwelcoming opening. In the distance, beyond the palace, can be seen a thin crescent moon shining in a black sky over the mountain peaks.

The Seven of Swords represents the application of mental energy in a cautious, wily and diplomatic way in order to gain the end desired. Here the message is brains rather than brawn, and life may require the individual to develop guile and wit and cunning. The feeling of the Seven of Swords is ambivalent, for we cannot be sure of the rightness or moral integrity of the goal; and certainly for Orestes, his motive for creeping back into Argos by stealth is a violent one. Yet he obeys the will of the radiant sun-god, although he is about to commit matricide. There is something slightly questionable about the Seven of Swords, even if the goal is apparently a 'good' or justified one, and this raises the problem of the essential amorality of the mind. Uncontaminated by feeling values, the intellect can be cold and manipulative, and the end can justify the means, even when that end is a noble one. But this card suggests that life may require us to develop such attributes, even if our natures dislike such obvious cunning. In order to achieve a goal, tact, deliberate charm, and even subterfuge may be necessary, and this leaves us with an uncomfortable feeling if we are at all ethical in our dealings with others.

But Orestes cannot arrive in Argos at the head of a parade with trumpets blaring. All that would happen would be that Clytemnestra and her lover would imprison and probably kill him, and he would be

THE SUIT OF SWORDS

blocked from accomplishing the god's will. Therefore he must compromise his character, and this seems to be a requirement of the stage of the journey reflected by the Seven of Swords. Guile is one of the attributes of the mind, and guile must therefore sometimes be used in life. In any exchange of opinions, this guile is needed; otherwise we should simply bully others and shout them down, and achieve nothing. Every politician understands this quality of guile; so too do priests and counsellors, for tact is the kinder face of guile, and ideas must be clothed tactfully if they are to be communicated – for good or ill.

On a divinatory level, the Seven of Swords heralds a time when it is necessary to use guile, tact, diplomacy, and wit rather than strong-armed bullying tactics to achieve one's ends. This may leave an uncomfortable feeling of falseness, but life may require it.

Eight of Swords

The card of the Eight of Swords portrays Orestes in a fearful posture, his hands up to fend off his doom. A ring of eight swords surrounds him, points embedded in the ground. To his left stands Apollo, looking stern and angry. To his right crouch the three Furies, robed in black, with white, ugly faces, snake-hair, and leathery bat-wings. In the distance, menacing clouds hang over the mountain peaks.

The Eight of Swords portrays a situation of bondage through fear. Unlike the paralysis of the Two, this bondage involves a full knowledge of the situation and the probable consequences of any choice. Here Orestes knows all too well what will happen if he murders his mother, or if he refuses to murder her; for either way, he loses. Thus he remains frozen, fending off the moment of choice. Although choices are not usually quite so florid as that of Orestes, nevertheless the Eight of Swords reflects a situation of paralyzing indecision. Part of the discomfort springs from the individual's awareness of exactly how he or she got into such a situation, but it is too late for regrets or backtracking. Unlike the blindness of the Two, the Eight portrays a painful consciousness of one's own part in creating the present mess. This is the moment before a difficult choice, exacerbated by the unpleasant realization that one has created the situation oneself.

There are many typical life situations where the bondage and paralysis of the Eight of Swords appear. One of the most characteristic is the problem of the individual who has been playing two people off against each other – a wife and a lover, a husband and a father, two friends – in an effort to fend off the day when some kind of choice and commitment must be made. Trying to keep one from finding out about the other may hold the problem of decision-making in abeyance for a time; but sooner or later there will be a confrontation, and then there is the moment of shock when one sees how one's subterfuges and delaying tactics have made the whole thing much worse. Thus the Eight of Swords emerges naturally from the Seven, as though guile and subtlety, although called upon for the best of reasons and necessary at the time, create their own snare. Then we must accept responsibility for the entire episode, try to understand what we truly want, and act once and for all. Thus a solution is possible.

On a divinatory level, the Eight of Swords heralds a situation where the individual is unable to act because of his or her fear of the consequences. A decision is necessary, but either choice will lead to trouble. There is a dawning realization that one has created the dilemma oneself, for there is usually a long past of avoidance, duplicity, blindness and fear of confrontation, often to 'avoid hurting' someone, which lies behind the present impasse. It is important to face honestly one's own part in the problem.

Nine of Swords

The card of the Nine of Swords portrays Orestes standing with his hands covering his ears. Behind him, the three Furies hover menacingly in a mass of grey cloud. Each holds three swords, and all nine swords point toward the young prince. Behind them the sky is black over the mountains.

THE SUIT OF SWORDS

The Nine of Swords reflects an experience of great fear and anxiety. This is the card of nightmare, the fantasy of impending doom that does not necessarily manifest as a concrete event but is frightening and painful because of the sheer power of the fantasy. Here Orestes has fulfilled his task and killed his mother, and now the Furies pursue him. But by their very nature they are not corporeal; they cannot physically harm him or strike him down. They torment him through guilt – through his fears and fantasies of destruction. The Nine of Swords might be called an image of what psychology calls free-floating anxiety, because it reflects a state where the individual expects a terrible future outcome even when there are no actual indications that such a bad future will truly manifest.

However our fears may vary from one person to another, many people – perhaps most – are afflicted from time to time by this nightmare anxiety of a terrible future. For some, it is the fear that a loved one will reject us, or die, or leave us for another. For many people it is the fear of financial catastrophe or loss, or the collapse of a creative project. Fear of future failure torments many, and so too does the terror of loneliness, illness, and isolated old age. The problem with such frightening visions of the future is that, if we are powerfully affected by them and begin to believe them, we act accordingly, and become suspicious and closed to life; thus destroying any possibility of future happiness and often creating the very fate we fear through our own suspicions. The Nine of Swords is a deeply psychological card, for these morbid fantasies of a doomed future often spring from guilt about the past – and such is the case with Orestes, for whom the Furies are a personification of his corrosive guilt. This guilt springs from the decision which is made in the Eight, and that in turn springs from the dilemma which the individual has created from choices in the past. Only insight symbolized by Athene, can dispel the tormenting fantasy of the Furies.

On a divinatory level, the Nine of Swords heralds a period of great anxiety and forboding about the future. It is important to examine

THE SUIT OF SWORDS

where guilt about the past might lie behind such fears, rather than being enslaved by them to one's future detriment.

Ten of Swords

The card of the Ten of Swords portrays the goddess Athene, standing calmly and holding in her right hand an upright sword. To her right crouch the three Furies, their menace contained within the ring of nine swords. To her left, Orestes lies unconscious on the ground, nearly spent. The black sky over the mountains gradually gives way to a rising sun, just visible on the horizon.

The Ten of Swords represents an ending, and here we see the ending of the ancient curse, accomplished through the judgement and fairness of the goddess of Justice. To Orestes, no hope is in sight; he is nearly dead of despair and exhaustion, and cannot see that his freedom has come at last. To the individual who has at last reached the end of something, where there is no hope left and only disillusionment and disappointment to take into the future, the experience of the Ten of Swords seems like a death. It is a black time, when we see something at last as it truly is, and recognize that there is nowhere further to go. But although Orestes is too sunk in his despair to witness it, the sun slowly rises in the distance, and a new beginning is heralded in the midst of the blackness of his defeat. The insight and clarity of Athene have disarmed the Furies, and in the story this occurs through the agency of a human jury. This suggests that what truly redeems us from our worst and most insoluble problem is not a lightning bolt from heaven, nor a magical piece of good luck, but the careful deliberation of the human mind with its great gift for impartial reflection. A family curse such as Orestes has to bear is an image of inner conflicts passed down from one generation to another, where the grandparents and parents have been unable to face life's conflicts honestly and the children must inevitably suffer until insight is gained.

Thus the Ten of Swords, although not exactly a fairy-tale happy ending, represents the proper and inevitable completion of a process which began with the birth of new ideas and perceptions of life in the Ace. Often such a birth means that some deep-seated and ancient problem is forced to the surface and something must ultimately leave our lives; and such separations are painful and difficult. But once the crisis is over, the sun can rise again, and we move on not merely disillusioned and disappointed, but freed of some deep canker which has its roots in a past older than ourselves, and which our own suffering has released and redeemed.

On a divinatory level, the Ten of Swords heralds the final ending of a difficult situation. The ending may be painful, but at last the situation is faced truthfully, and a new future, with fewer conflicts, can begin.

THE SUIT OF SWORDS

The Court Cards

| PAGE OF SWORDS | KNIGHT OF SWORDS | QUEEN OF SWORDS | KING OF SWORDS |

Page of Swords

The card of the Page of Swords portrays a youth, dressed in a pale blue tunic, kneeling among the clouds in a turbulent sky. His fair hair streams out into the wind which emerges from his mouth as he violently blows. In his hand he holds a silver sword. Below him can be seen a grey mountainous landscape.

Here, in the card of the Page of Swords, we meet the nascent, unformed and primitive beginnings of the element of air: the first stirrings of independent mental activity and formulation. This is embodied in the mythic figure of Zephyrus, the youthful ruler of the West Wind. The Empire of the Four Winds sprang from the union of Eos, goddess of the dawn, and Astraeus, a personification of the starry night sky. Notus was the South Wind, and Eurus the East Wind; but the two most powerful children of the union of dawn and night sky were Boreas, the North Wind and Zephyrus. Together these two brothers were worshipped as savage and baleful forces of nature, immature and unbridled, who took pleasure in brewing storms and tossing the waves of the sea. Elemental in disposition, Zephyrus lived with his brother Boreas in the mountainous caves of Thrace, and mounted the

THE SUIT OF SWORDS

clouds to blow out of his mouth the threatening West Wind. The youth was possessed of a spiteful and malicious nature. From his union with the hideous Harpy, Podarge – a creature with a woman's head and breasts, and the wings and claws of a bird – were born the two wild horses which drew the chariot of the hero Achilles during the Trojan War.

But later Zephyrus' disposition softened, although his brother's did not. This was perhaps because the West Wind was given as a bride the beautiful and gentle Iris, female messenger of the gods and guardian of the rainbow, whom we met in the Major Arcana card of Temperance. From the effects of this union Zephyrus eventually transformed into a sweet-scented wind which gently fanned the blessed regions of Elysium where the souls of the heroes dwelt in eternal tranquility.

Zephyrus, the Page of Swords, is an image of the first primitive stirrings of an independent mental life, which must emerge first in its childlike form before we can begin to formulate our own ideas and concepts and express these to others. Because he is young and elemental, the Page of Swords is querulous, and like any child can be prone to cruel gossip, mockery, rudeness and general mischievousness – a kind of playful exercise of the powers of thought and speech before any feeling values or ethical codes intervene to shape and direct the mental activity. This early stirring of original and independent thought can emerge as a propensity for petty quarrels, and as an invasive curiosity which does not respect the privacy of its object. In just this spirit, Zephyrus, ruler of the West Wind, enjoys brewing storms and tossing the sea, not because he is evil, but because he is so curious to see what happens. The speech of children is notoriously cruel, but this cruelty is only deeply hurtful if we have something to hide, or if our pride or self-image cannot take the pummelling.

Gossip is truly the realm of the Page of Swords, for gossip is our adult equivalent of this child-spirit playing with a baleful elemental force. Gossip can wound, and even, given time, exaggeration and the right ears, become powerfully destructive to reputation and relationship. 'Did you hear...?' says the gossip, and before much longer the tale has been twisted, embellished, fed on envy and spite, and eventually turns into a great tempest, transformed beyond all recognition from the little wind emerging from the mouth of Zephyrus. We all have this propensity for gossip within us, and it springs from a kind of elemental curiosity about others. Gossip is a great leveller, and no one is immune from it – least of all the person who believes his or her life to be blameless, for where Zephyrus cannot find something out, he will make it up instead. The Page of Swords is thus a highly ambivalent card, because its raw childlike energy marks the beginning of true independent thought; but at the same time, Zephyrus can be spiteful and malicious, and the petty quarrels which are his trademark can turn unpleasant and mushroom into big winds. The energy of Zephyrus needs to be nurtured and directed without being crushed, for he embodies our childlike curiosity about life, the world and people.

When the Page of Swords appears in a spread, it is time to meet within oneself the childlike curiosity and potential for spiteful gossip which the Page embodies, and which marks the beginning of the use of mental powers. One may oneself be the victim of others' gossip; or there can be a tendency to start petty quarrels and to be irritable and difficult. But these things reflect the emergence of new ideas and true independent thinking – often in one who has been accustomed to accepting the views of others.

Knight of Swords

The card of the Knight of Swords portrays a pair of young men, identical twins, clothed in pale grey tunics and silver armour, with silver helmets over their fair hair. Each holds a silver sword, and both are mounted on the back of a single pale grey horse. The horse is agitated, its front legs outstretched as though about to take off in flight, and the twins hold their swords aloft as though ready for battle. Above horse and riders the grey sky is turbulent, with scudding clouds.

Here, in the card of the Knight of Swords, we meet the flexible, volatile and changeable dimension of the

THE SUIT OF SWORDS

element of air, which is constantly in motion. This turbulent activity in the realm of the mind is embodied in the mythic figures of the quarrelsome Dioscuri, the Warrior Twins, who were called Castor and Polydeuces. Their mother was Leda, queen of Sparta, who was pursued by the amorous Zeus, king of the gods. When she refused the god's advances, he transformed himself into a swan and raped her. She was already pregnant by her husband King Tyndareos, and bore two eggs by her swan-lover. Out of one were hatched two mortal children, Castor and his sister Clytemnestra, whom we have already met in the story of Orestes in the numbered cards of the Suit of Swords. Out of the other egg came the two divine children of Zeus, Polydeuces and Helen, whom we met in the Minor Arcana card of the Queen of Cups. Thus the Dioscuri were twin brothers, but Castor was mortal and Polydeuces divine.

The Dioscuri, who were never separated from one another in any adventure, became the pride of Sparta. Castor was famous as a soldier and tamer of horses, Polydeuces as a boxer. Both were pugnacious and known for their propensity to start quarrels. They eventually quarrelled with another pair of twins, called Idas and Lynceus. Idas killed Castor, the mortal twin, and Polydeuces in turn killed Lynceus with his spear. Zeus, intervening on behalf of his son, struck Idas dead with a thunderbolt. Polydeuces was grief-stricken at the loss of his brother, and prayed to his father Zeus that he might not outlive him. He refused immortality unless Castor might share it with him. Zeus therefore allowed them both to spend their days alternately in the divine abode of Olympus and beneath the earth in Hades' realm; and he set their images among the stars as the Twins.

The Dioscuri are images of an abrupt and mercurial energy, the capacity of the human mind to be suddenly inspired or taken over by a new idea which throws the old order into chaos and leaves changes in its wake. The duality of the heavenly Twins suggests a duality or duplicity in this realm of the mind, because often these sudden new ideas which break in upon our humdrum lives either inaugurate conflict or are themselves ambivalent and full of conflict. The pugnacity

THE SUIT OF SWORDS

and callousness of the Dioscuri also tell us something about the quality of mental energy described by the Knight of Swords: It takes no account of human feeling, and is often the cause of relationships being disrupted or severed because the individual is suddenly possessed by an idea which demands his or her hurting another. Thus there is a basic attitude inherent in the Knight of Swords, which is not unlike the figure of Don Juan in romantic legend. This figure is intensely attractive because of his brilliance, but he is callous; he has no real feeling for the continuity of the past and the integrity of human relationship, and is not prepared to make personal sacrifices or compromise the cool and lofty vision of the moment.

In ordinary life we may see the energy of the Dioscuri at work when an individual abandons responsibilities and ties in order to pursue some new and youthful adventure. In psychology, this impulse is called the *puer aeternus*, the eternal youth, and it is an impulse which is more dominant in some people than in others. The spirit of the Knight of Swords cannot bear to grow old, or stagnate in too much bondage. Prolonged intimacy makes him fidget, and he needs constant mental stimuli in order to avoid becoming bored. He possesses the peculiar double face of being both destructive to feeling ties and of creatively catapulting an individual out of boredom and bondage into new phases of growth, which often necessitates a broken heart or two. Thus he serves both a negative and a positive function at the same time – reflected here in the image of the Twins. To the Dioscuri, conflict and movement are natural, and one cannot spend too long feeling guilty about who might be hurt when the mind abruptly turns and moves in a new direction. The quicksilver quality of the Twins is reflected in the image by the agitation of the horse, which hardly touches the ground and which cannot remain still, bearing its twin riders onward toward new adventures.

When the Knight of Swords appears in a spread, it is time for the individual to be prepared for sudden changes which break apart the ordinary patterns of life. These changes may be inaugurated by an individual coming into one's life who possesses the quicksilver,

THE SUIT OF SWORDS

fascinating and disruptive qualities of the Dioscuri; or it may take the form of a new idea or vision which erupts from within oneself and which throws ordinary life into disorder for a time. Thus, whether the Knight of Swords appears from without or within, his gift is the ability to move with changes, and the turbulence which he brings may ultimately lead to a broader vision of life.

Queen of Swords

The card of the Queen of Swords portrays a cool, stern-faced yet beautiful woman with pale hair, severely dressed in a simple pale blue robe. She wears a golden crown, and is seated on a silver throne. In one hand she holds a silver sword; in the other, a jug from which water spills onto the ground. Behind her a vista of snow-capped mountains can be seen beneath a still, cool blue sky.

Here, in the card of the Queen of Swords, we meet the stable, reflective, contained dimension of the element of air. This is embodied in the mythic figure of Atalanta the Huntress, who was disappointed in love through having too high ideals. Atalanta, whose name means 'unswaying', was the child of King Iasus, who had wished passionately for a male heir. Atalanta's birth disappointed him so cruelly that he exposed her on a hillside near Calydon, but the child was rescued and suckled by a bear which the moon-goddess Artemis-Hecate sent to her aid. Atalanta grew to womanhood among a clan of hunters who found and reared her. But she remained a virgin and always carried arms, and she was not yet reconciled to her father, who refused to acknowledge her.

Atalanta achieved many famous deeds of arms, including the famous Calydonian boar-hunt where she fought alongside the men and achieved the first strike at the boar. But although the young hero Meleager, son of the war-god Ares and the best javelin-thrower in Greece, fell in love with her, Atalanta refused to succumb to an ordinary woman's fate. Eventually her father, proud of her prowess, recognized

THE SUIT OF SWORDS

her at last, and promised to find her a noble husband. But she protested, saying: 'Father, I consent on one condition. Any suitor for my hand must either beat me in a foot race, or else let me kill him.' Many unfortunate princes lost their lives in consequence, because she was the swiftest mortal alive. But eventually a young man called Melanion invoked Aphrodite's assistance. The goddess gave him three golden apples, telling him to delay Atalanta by letting them fall, one after another, in the course of the race. The stratagem was successful, and the marriage took place. But it was doomed, for Melanion persuaded Atalanta to lie with him in a sacred precinct of Zeus, and the god, angry at the sacrilege, turned them both into lions; and as the Greeks believed, lions do not mate with lions, but only with leopards, and they were thus prevented from ever again enjoying each other.

Atalanta, the Queen of Swords, is an image of the aloofness and untouchability of the mind, which can hold to an ideal of perfection to the extent that all sensual concerns are excluded or devalued. The figure of the Queen of Swords is a cool one, because her perfectionism and her identification with the masculine world of the mind and spirit fit her for friendship but not for erotic love. Thus the Queen of Swords is a regal and dignified figure, but also a lonely one, and this loneliness, although often borne with pride and integrity, springs less from circumstances than from a reluctance to allow anything too human to mar the ideal of perfection. The idealism of the Queen of Swords is lofty and noble, and there is a loyalty which can withstand many of life's most difficult tests. But it is an idealism which permits no human failing. The myth of Atalanta may be found in many of our popular fairy tales, in the image of the cool princess who demands that her suitors attempt impossible tasks in order to win her. This demand may be subtle and even unconscious, and it may drive love out of one's life. It can also be a creative demand, because it spurs both the individual and others to become more than they are. But it is a chill and lonely vision, for no suitor – or oneself – can ultimately pass the impossible test except in fairy tales, and those who identify with Atalanta in real life tend to wait forever while mortal life passes by and the water of feeling spills from the jug, wasted, on to the ground. Thus the Queen of Swords, who possesses the priceless virtues of loyalty and integrity and the capacity to bear sorrow without breaking, is ultimately an image of emotional frustration and isolation, because she is untouchable.

Just as the King of Cups is an ambivalent figure because the masculine role of kingship sits uncomfortably beside the essentially feminine element of water, the Queen of Swords is likewise ambivalent because the feminine role of queenship sits uncomfortably beside the essentially masculine element of air. The myth of Atalanta tells us something deep and subtle about the psychology of the Queen of Swords, for her father wished for a male child and refused to accept her value as a woman; only when she had proven herself through a man's feats of arms did he acknowledge her. The striving toward perfection which is expressed in the image of the Queen of Swords is in some ways an effort to prove oneself to a father-god who is ultimately always beyond one's reach, for one is never quite good enough simply because one is made of flesh. Thus the Queen of Swords will accept nothing less than perfection because she herself has been expected to be perfect and failed.

When the Queen of Swords appears in a spread, it is time for the individual to meet that dimension of himself or herself which clings unswaying to an immovable faith in high ideals. These ideals may be noble and lofty, and help to improve consciousness and the quality of life. But they may also reject life, and be a defense against the fear of being human and therefore vulnerable to hurt. The individual needs to see where he or she might create problems through demanding superhuman perfection of others or oneself. If the Queen of Swords enters one's life as a strong, idealistic, aloof woman, it may be seen as a catalyst through which one discovers this aspect of oneself.

King of Swords

The card of the King of Swords portrays a handsome man with chiselled features and fair hair and beard, robed in grey and crowned with gold. He is seated on a silver throne

THE SUIT OF SWORDS

whose arms are engraved with the emblem of perfect harmony, the equilateral triangle. In one hand he holds a silver sword; in the other, a pair of scales. Behind him stretches a landscape of mountain peaks beneath a cloudy grey sky.

Here, in the card of the King of Swords, we meet the dynamic, initiating, organizing dimension of the element of air. This is embodied in the mythic figure of the hero Odysseus, who was called 'the Wily One', and whom we have met briefly in the Minor Arcana card of the Queen of Wands, as the husband of Penelope. Odysseus, king of Ithaca, had been secretly begotten by Sisyphus on the daughter of the thief Autolycus. Thus he inherited some of the guile and cleverness of his father. With the outbreak of the Trojan War, Odysseus joined the other Greek princes in the assault on Troy; and he proved over and over to be a shrewd advisor and a sound strategist. It was Odysseus who first conceived the idea of the Trojan Horse, that huge hollow wooden beast which was sent into the city as a gift to the goddess Athene, and which was secretly filled with Greek troops. But when Troy was finally sacked, Odysseus always showed mercy to the captives, and promised fair treatment to those who surrendered peaceably.

Despite his successes during the Trojan War, Odysseus was not so lucky on his return to Ithaca. For ten years he was forced to wander, driven by gales and forced to contend with strange and dangerous foes throughout the lands which he visited. Among these places were the Island of the Lotus-Eaters, where his men became drugged and lost their memory; the Island of the Cyclopes, where ferocious one-eyed giants, sons of the smith-god Hephaistos, threatened to kill them; and the Island of Dawn, ruled by Circe the sorceress, where Odysseus' crew were turned into pigs. He had to sail his ship between the terrifying sea-monsters Scylla and Charybdis, and escaped the alluring calls of the Sirens who sang men to their deaths beneath the sea; and through all these trials he acted with foresight, cleverness, strategy and guile, driven by his determination to reach his homeland despite the opportunities for love, wealth and power which came his way during his wanderings.

THE SUIT OF SWORDS

Odysseus, the King of Swords, is an image of the strategic skills of the human mind at their most impressive. Of all the heroes in Greek myth, Odysseus is the most brilliant and the most inventive, although not always the most honest, for his intellectual gifts made him a talented liar. But his craftiness was never malicious; it was always used in the service of those principles he held sacred – the triumph of the Greeks over the Trojans, and the sanctity of his homeland, his wife and his son Telemachus. The King of Swords is a man of principles, although these principles sometimes lack the depth of feeling which might relate to an individual situation rather than a general law. Thus Odysseus, in his dealings with his fellows, made many enemies, because his principles were often ill-suited to the actual situation he faced with his fellows. The figure of the King of Swords has high ideals about decency, kindness and fairness, and Odysseus' behaviour to the defeated Trojans reflects these principles. But his kindness is cool and not really built upon true emotional response. Although many women fell in love with Odysseus, he never responded in any other than a sexual way. Thus he comes down to us in myth as a brilliant strategist, a clever bargainer and manipulator, a kind man with high ideals, and a chill figure with no real empathy for other individuals. Odysseus is the image of the wanderer, not in the sense that the Knight of Swords wanders after adventure, but in the sense that he is not rooted in the heart and is therefore not rooted in relationship with others. His wanderings may be taken as a kind of inner homelessness, a lack of connectedness which is more than compensated by his decency and intelligence, but which isolates him from his fellows and disappoints those who love him.

The King of Swords embodies a quality of intellectual leadership which is attractive and dynamic in the world. His ambivalence lies in his tendency to dissociation from feeling, which can cause him to seem rather shallow and untrustworthy. This is his paradox: that he is a man of unquestionably high principles, yet at the same time a person who, like the proverbial weathercock, can shift unexpectedly from one allegiance to another in order to preserve diplomacy and cooperation. Although this is a contradiction in terms, both the noble and guileful aspects of his nature spring from the same idealistic root.

THE SUIT OF SWORDS

When the King of Swords appears in a spread, it is time to meet within oneself the ambivalent gift of intellectual leadership and strategy. Intellectual prowess and inspired ideas about how to develop things in the future are qualities which he possesses in abundance. Sometimes this figure can appear in one's life in the form of an individual who is striking by virtue of his mental gifts and his capacity to innovate changes in the world. But if such an individual enters one's sphere it may be seen as a catalyst through whom one can contact this dimension of oneself.

ACE OF PENTACLES
TWO OF PENTACLES
THREE OF PENTACLES
FOUR OF PENTACLES
FIVE OF PENTACLES
SIX OF PENTACLES
SEVEN OF PENTACLES
EIGHT OF PENTACLES
NINE OF PENTACLES
TEN OF PENTACLES

THE SUIT OF PENTACLES

The Numbered Cards

The story of Daedalus, the Athenian craftsman who built the Labyrinth for King Minos of Crete, is a subtle tale, and its hero is painted in many hues; for he is neither a wholly good man nor a villian, but a curious mixture of both. This story, with its ingenious and amoral protagonist, befits the Suit of Pentacles, for it illustrates the problems, challenges, aspirations, pitfalls and complex morality of earthly endeavour with its failures and rewards.

Daedalus was descended from the royal house of Athens, and was a wonderful smith, having been instructed by the goddess Athene herself. He spent his early years perfecting his skills, and it was said that he invented the saw and the axe, as well as being the first man to fix arms and legs to the shapeless primitive statues of the gods. Still in his prime, he became renowned for his ingenuity and cunning.

This early success, however, was doomed by the craftsman's own flawed character. Daedalus had a nephew called Talos, and this Talos, although only twelve years old, began to surpass his gifted uncle in the art of creating tools and beautiful objects. Talos invented the potter's wheel and the compass while still a child. Daedalus grew unbearably jealous and was torn by conflict, for while he loved and admired his nephew he was an ambitious man and could not tolerate his own reputation being threatened in such a way; so he murdered Talos by throwing the boy from the roof of Athene's temple. Caught in the act of trying to hide the body, Daedalus was condemned, but managed to flee Athens before any punishment could be visited upon him.

The smith landed in Crete, and sought and received the protection of King Minos. For some time he lived in high favour at Knossos, Minos' capital, creating architectural beauties for the king and amusing the palace children with ingenious toys. But then a bad fate befell King Minos, which we have glimpsed already in the story behind the Major Arcana card of the Tower; for Minos offended the god Poseidon by refusing to sacrifice a white bull on the god's altar, and Poseidon retaliated by afflicting Minos' wife Pasiphae with a violent passion for the bull. Pasiphae, driven by her shameful compulsion, appealed to Daedalus, and begged him to contrive a way in which she might meet and couple with the bull in secret. Thus Daedalus was caught once again in a conflict, for Minos was his protector and patron, yet it was clear that the hand of the god lay on Pasiphae.

Daedalus chose the god, and constructed a wooden cow in which Pasiphae crouched and mated with the bull. When the hideous Minotaur, with a bull's head and a man's body, was born from this union, King Minos, ignorant of the part which Daedalus had played in its conception, begged the smith to build a hiding-place in which the monster could be concealed. Daedalus agreeably served his master once more, and constructed the tortuous corridors of the Labyrinth, in which, once a man entered, he was irretrievably lost. But when the hero Theseus arrived in Crete to slay the Minotaur, and Minos' daughter Ariadne fell in love with him, it was to Daedalus that she turned to find a way for Theseus to enter the Labyrinth and trace his steps safely out again. Daedalus again betrayed his master, and made for Ariadne a ball of golden thread, one end of which she held, while the young hero entered the dark corridors holding the other, slew the Minotaur, and followed the golden thread out into the sunlight again.

This time Minos discovered the treachery of his craftsman, and locked Daedalus in the Labyrinth. But the smith ingeniously made a pair of wings from beeswax and wood and feathers which the sympathetic Pasiphae brought him, and flew from one of the towers, borne by the wind toward safe shores. Eventually he landed in Cumae on the coast of Italy, and from there made his way to Sicily, where he gained the favour of King Cocalus.

King Minos pursued him, and tracked him all over Greece and Italy. The king carried with him a triton shell, and wherever he went he promised to reward richly anyone who could pass a linen thread through it – a feat which he knew Daedalus alone could perform. In this way he found the smith's hiding-place, but King Cocalus refused to part with his valued guest. Cocalus ordered his daughters to pour boiling water into Minos' bath, and Daedalus thus lived into contented and wealthy old age.

THE SUIT OF PENTACLES

Ace of Pentacles

The card of the Ace of Pentacles portrays a swarthy and powerfully built figure with long curling brown hair and a fish's tail, rising out of the depths of the sea and bearing aloft a single golden pentacle. Around him lie crags draped in vines richly hung with ripening grapes, while in the distance can be seen a landscape of fertile green hills opening out on to a bay.

Here we meet the god Poseidon, whom we encountered earlier in the Major Arcana card of the Tower. Poseidon was the son of Cronos and Rhea, and shared the fate of his brothers and sisters: at birth he was swallowed by his father. He was disgorged with the others when Zeus gave Cronos the draught which made him vomit up his other children. After their common victory over Cronos, the paternal heritage was divided into three parts. Zeus took the vast heavens, Hades the murky underworld, and Poseidon the seas, lakes and rivers and the surface of the earth itself, since earth was sustained by his waters and he could shake it at will. He became notorious among the gods because of his craving for land, and fell into conflict with many of them due to his efforts to appropriate islands and pieces of the mainland of Greece.

Poseidon was a fertility god, husband of the great Earth Mother and lord of the physical universe. He was honoured in the form of a bull and was called 'earth-shaker', a great black beast with glittering red eyes who lived in the bowels of the earth and stamped his feet, causing the mountains to move and the seas to flood the land. Thus Poseidon is a raw force of nature, and in the Ace of Pentacles we encounter his power as a burst of new energy for material creation. Where the Ace of Wands rises upward as the birth of a new creative vision, the Ace of Pentacles turns its immense creative potency downward into the world, and it is this fresh emerging need to concretize and create in the manifest world that stands behind all our material ambitions. The individual who can manifest money and make things happen on a worldly level experiences something of the power of this ancient earthy god, and the Ace of

THE SUIT OF PENTACLES

Pentacles heralds the eruption of fresh ambition toward material creation and success.

On a divinatory level, the Ace of Pentacles augurs the possibility of material achievement, because the raw energy for this kind of work is now available to the individual. Often money is made available through a legacy or some other source, coupled with the ingenuity and persistance to utilize these resources effectively.

Two of Pentacles

The card of the Two of Pentacles portrays Daedalus, a swarthy, brown-haired man, wearing an ochre-coloured tunic and a brown leather apron, in his workshop. Before him stands his work-table, supported by two golden pentacles. On either side of him on a wooden trellis cluster vines heavy with grapes, and in the background can be seen a landscape of rich green hills. In his left hand Daedalus holds an axe, which he has just invented. In his right hand, he holds a saw, also his invention. Before him on the table are spread the tools of his trade.

The image of the Two of Pentacles portrays Daedalus at the beginning of his climb, where he develops his skills and builds his reputation among the Athenians, applying his ingenuity toward new inventions, investing effort in new projects, keeping himself busy and active and willing to try several things at once. Here we see the picture of a materially ambitious man who is still open to new creative ideas and is willing to take risks to utilize his talents. This flexibility can vanish all too quickly when we have become immured in a successful structure which we have built, but it is always there at the beginning, and can, when the Two of Pentacles appears, be regained.

Thus the Two of Pentacles represents a state of change or fluctuation in material fortunes. This fluctuation does not imply loss, however, but rather a flow of creative energy outward into many projects. Here the raw power of the Ace has polarized, as with all the Twos of the Minor

Arcana, and the drive for material creation must be grounded and channelled. The old saying, 'Money makes money', is highly appropriate for this card, for it is necessary to take risks and use capital so that it can work to produce before any real gains are made. The Two of Pentacles demands flexibility and a willingness to put money and energy to work, and often this means juggling and shifting resources in a manner which to the more staid in nature seems unnecessarily risky and anxiety-provoking. Yet the Two of Pentacles may be seen as a 'good' card because, although it suggests the necessity of a certain light-footedness in financial matters, it promises rewards because creative energy is put to work.

On a divinatory level, the Two of Pentacles heralds a time when money and energy are likely to be available for new projects that might lead to a rewarding future; but the individual must be willing to put his resources to work, taking risks and using capital, rather than hoarding and saving at a time when new opportunities arise. Thus the Two of Pentacles is likely to be a welcome card to those who know how to 'play' with money.

Three of Pentacles

The card of the Three of Pentacles portrays Daedalus standing on a raised platform or dais, still clothed in his ochre tunic and leather apron. Three Athenians stand before him, dressed in subtle but rich robes. Each offers him a golden pentacle. Around the four men, vines hang laden on a trellis, and a background of green hills can be seen against a clear blue sky.

The Three of Pentacles, in common with the other Threes in the Minor Arcana, implies an initial completion, and here we see Daedalus receiving the early rewards for his labours. The initial completion here represents the first stages of concretization of a project, rather like the completed shell of a building before any internal structures or decoration have been developed. Daedalus has achieved a firm position at the beginning of his career, although it remains to be seen whether he can strengthen this position and make it permanent. As we know from the myth, he cannot. Thus the initial completion of the Three of Pentacles is not the final stage of a project. There may be hard work, difficulty and risk before one can count oneself materially secure.

There is cause for celebration in the Three of Pentacles, but this celebration should be taken with a full awareness of the work to come. In the story of Daedalus, the factor which causes the collapse of this early success is not a material one, but a flaw in the character of the man himself. This also needs to be considered when we evaluate the meaning of the numbered cards in the Suit of Pentacles, for the material rewards which this Suit promises are contingent not only upon shrewd business skills and willingness to work hard, but also upon character. An individual's inability to know his own limits, or his belief that he can do whatever he pleases in the material world regardless of the consequences to others, is often the fatal flaw which eventually leads to the collapse of the early success indicated by the Three. Therefore the message of this card is: Enjoy the early fruits of your labours, but consider the future, not only in terms of the work which must be done, but in terms of your own capacity to handle it.

On a divinatory level, the Three of Pentacles heralds a time of early success in some material endeavour. A project may earn profits, or a creative venture such as a book may show early success in the market. But as with all the Threes, this is not a final resolution, but a stage which will hopefully lead through hard work and difficulty to a more permanent reward.

Four of Pentacles

The card of the Four of Pentacles portrays Daedalus clutching four golden pentacles tightly in his arms. He stares angrily at a boy who is busy at the work-table – his

THE SUIT OF PENTACLES

nephew Talos, clothed in a pale green tunic, brown-haired and dark-complexioned, concentrating on a beautiful golden ornament which he is in process of completing. Around both the artisan and his nephew, richly-laden vines twine up a trellis, while green hills can be seen in the distance against a clear sky.

The Four of Pentacles is sometimes called the card of the miser, because it implies a condition of being too anxiously attached to one's money or worldly position. Because of this tight grasp, the flow of energy which is always necessary in the Suit of Pentacles to develop material success is dammed up and begins to stagnate. Here we see Daedalus responding in anger and jealousy to his gifted nephew, who has already surpassed him in skills although the boy is only twelve years old. Rather than meeting this competitive challenge in a more creative way, Daedalus has chosen to react by trying to cling too tightly to the situation of the past. This leads eventually to the destruction not only of Talos, but of Daedalus himself.

The Four of Pentacles is not only concerned with holding on to one's money with too tight a grasp. Money is a symbol as well as an objective reality, for it is through money that we assert our evaluation of things. Thus it embodies our own worth, the price we set upon our self-expression. The rewards which a person expects for his skills also represent an estimation of how much his skills are worth in terms of value, and because we so often fail to understand the deeper meaning of money in our lives, we assume that money itself is responsible for most of the world's ills. Spiritual and esoteric teachings suggest that money is intrinsically evil and corrupts; but these teachings do not draw the distinction between the actual object and the emotional value we place on it. Thus Daedalus' jealousy is not really about the business he might lose because his nephew can create prettier objects, for one might assume that the Athenian market is big enough for them both; besides which, he might have used the challenge of Talos as a spur to further develop his own talents. But the jealousy points to a problem in self-value, for Daedalus' estimation of himself is embedded in what he makes, and the loss of one is also the loss of the other.

THE SUIT OF PENTACLES

Thus the Four of Pentacles is a subtle card, for it is not only about an attitude of miserliness which causes the individual to cling too tightly to his resources, thereby causing the stagnation of energy and the inability to make future gains. This card also describes an inner problem of not enough confidence, and a fear of letting go which can result not only in material but also in emotional stagnation. Letting emotional energy flow freely goes hand in hand with letting material resources flow, and the person who clings too tightly, who cannot delegate authority, who hoards his praise and generosity, creates internal as well as external blockage.

On a divinatory level, the Four of Pentacles warns about an attitude of holding too tightly to things which are bound up with one's sense of self-value. The fear of loss may mean no loss, but it also means no gain, for there is a stagnation of creative energy which can eventually not only block funds but also block self-expression.

Five of Pentacles

The card of the Five of Pentacles portrays Daedalus, shrouded in a tattered brown cloak, creeping away by night from the city where only a short time before he had achieved such acclaim. On a hill behind him stands his workshop, its trellis adorned with vines and displaying five golden pentacles – the success which Daedalus must now leave behind him. The road on which he travels leads toward a barren landscape of brown hills. In the black sky a thin waning moon can be seen.

The Five of Pentacles is a card of loss, and we can see how it follows naturally upon the negative response to challenge portrayed in the Four. Because Daedalus could not adjust to the challenge of competition, he tried to cling to the position of the past, and this necessitated the murder of his talented nephew as the only solution. Now he flees Athens as a pauper, leaving behind him all the rewards of his years of hard work.

The Five of Pentacles often indicates the danger of a period of financial loss. But more importantly, it implies a loss of faith in oneself. Because we so often confuse self-value with material security, financial setbacks can destroy not only material confidence but also the individual's sense of direction and faith in himself or herself. During the disastrous American stock market crash of 1929, many individuals reacted to the financial catastrophe by committing suicide – a harsh response, if we consider how precious a human life is, yet a comprehensible one if we think of how totally many individuals identify their worth with their material success. The message of the Five of Pentacles is to let go, because if material disaster comes then perhaps it is in some way necessary, and the inevitable outgrowth of a wrong or inappropriate attitude. In the myth, Daedalus' collapse occurs because there is a fatal flaw in his character, and his loss may perhaps be the only possible way in which he can honestly confront that in him which is his own worst enemy. If material difficulties can be considered in this way, then the problems reflected by the Five of Pentacles can ultimately result in a transformation of the inner individual, so that the future can yield not only renewed material success but also a more solid inner centre which can cope with the challenges which success brings.

On a divinatory level, the Five of Pentacles augurs a period of financial difficulty or loss. This may be accompanied by a loss of faith in oneself, and it is important to try to respond to the challenge not only by letting go if necessary and preparing to begin again, but also by considering where one's own nature might have led to or exacerbated the problem. A reorientation is now possible not only on a financial level but also on an inner one.

Six of Pentacles

The card of the Six of Pentacles portrays Daedalus on his knees in homage, hands clasped in a gesture of supplication. Seated before him on a golden throne, there is King Minos of Crete – a mature man with black hair and beard and a swarthy complexion, robed in regal purple and wearing a golden crown. In his hands the king holds six golden pentacles, offering them to Daedalus in a promise of future patronage. Behind the kneeling craftsman and the enthroned king can be seen the walls of Minos' palace, decorated with painted friezes of bull-dancers and borders of grape-laden vines.

The Six of Pentacles is a harmonious card, reflecting the renewal of faith which here accompanies Daedalus' successful flight to Crete and his reward of the powerful and wealthy King Minos' patronage. After the catastrophe of the Five of Pentacles, with its implications of loss not only of possessions but of trust in life and one's own capabilities, the Six of Pentacles promises a kind of restoration through the generosity or charity of others. The atmosphere of this card is not one of reward for hard work, but rather of benevolence. One can sometimes count on the bounty of life, which is not always unkind and which will ultimately, in some way, recompense the individual for efforts made. Sometimes this experience of life's generosity arises from within the individual himself or herself, rather than through the charity of others; one discovers that one can still give without conditions even though one has suffered reversals and losses. The deeper meaning of the Six of Pentacles therefore touches on an important facet of the world of creation in form, because not everything is a result of conscious will or error. Sometimes good luck crosses one's path, and although one cannot plan for or expect this, nevertheless it often occurs just when our fortunes are at their lowest. Daedalus is not a wholly bad man, although he has committed a great crime. He is an ambivalent man, capable of much good as well as much evil, and life therefore does not judge him in the way in which society – embodied by the angry Athenians – might judge him. He has suffered for his crime by poverty and exile and humiliation, and now a new cycle begins, heralded by one of those strokes of good fortune which display themselves in kindness and generosity – one's own or another's.

On a divinatory level, the Six of Pentacles augurs a situation where there is money or substance to be shared, and where the individual will himself or herself be called upon to offer generosity or be the recipient of another's generosity. Faith in life and in one's capacities is regained.

Seven of Pentacles

The card of the Seven of Pentacles portrays Daedalus in the palace of King Minos. To his right, mounted on a painted column upon which his hand rests possessively, are six golden pentacles. To his left stands Queen Pasiphae, Minos' wife, clothed in purple robes and wearing a golden crown on her long brown hair. She wears an expression of anguish and desperation on her face, and offers the craftsman a single golden pentacle. Behind her can be seen the head and shoulders of a white bull.

The Seven of Pentacles portrays the situation of a difficult decision. Here we see Daedalus in a position of material security and royal favour, represented by the six golden pentacles beside him. He has worked long and hard to achieve his place at Minos' court, and can be justifiably proud of the new edifice he has built from the ruin embodied in the Five and the lucky gesture of benevolence implied by the Six. But now a new factor has entered the story: a proposition which might turn out to be even better in its rewards than the old, or which might turn out to precipitate even worse ruin. To side with Queen Pasiphae means to betray his patron; yet it also means following the will of the god Poseidon, who, being a god, might in the end turn out to be a far more sensible choice of ally.

Translated into more ordinary terms, the choice of Daedalus portrayed in the Seven of Pentacles reflects a situation where we are called upon to decide between the security of what we have already built and the shaky, uncertain possibilities of a new direction which may or may not lead to future success. One pole represents the safe choice, although there is implied in such safety the danger of stagnation and even misfortune if something 'divinely inspired' is rejected in favour of what is secure but lacking in vitality. The other pole represents something possibly risky, even dangerous, perhaps 'immoral' in the sense that it flies in the face of popular opinion. Yet this dangerous new possibility contains a life-force and potential for growth which might far outweigh the rewards of the secure path. Thus the Seven embodies a situation which sooner or later comes to every individual who attempts to manifest creative energy in the world. The hoped-for success may be achieved, but along with it the youthful spirit of the gamble is often lost, and there may be a limit to what one can accomplish through one channel alone. The problem is whether or not to take the new opportunity and risk losing all that has been built.

On a divinatory level, the Seven of Pentacles augurs a time when a difficult work decision must be made. Care and forethought are needed, and the question arises of whether to continue to develop what one has already built, or to put energy into a new project.

Eight of Pentacles

The card of the Eight of Pentacles portrays Daedalus at his workshop in the precincts of King Cocalus' palace in Sicily. On either side of him, richly laden vines clamber up wooden posts. Behind him can be seen a verdant vista of green mountains leading to the sea. On the ground at the craftsman's feet lie seven golden pentacles, all in an unfinished state and awaiting future work. On the wooden table before him lies a single golden pentacle, around which Daedalus engraves an elaborate border.

The Eight of Pentacles presents Daedalus once again as an apprentice, working hard on developing his skills. Implied here is the natural outcome of the Seven: Daedalus has chosen the god, and consequently a new venture has opened up to him, where new skills must be acquired so that the project may blossom and bear fruit. The Eight of Pentacles is the card of the apprentice, but unlike the Two, where we saw the craftsman juggling his energies and developing his talents through clever shifting of funds and resources, the Eight does not imply instability. Here we see a spirit of dedication and one-pointed energy. This enthusiastic spirit is often the accompaniment of a new venture, particularly if this is a departure from what we have done before. In many ways the Eight coincides with that period in life which follows what psychology calls 'mid-life crisis', for the Seven of Pentacles in some ways embodies just this crisis: What we have been has become stale, yet a departure into new pastures is often attended by anxiety and a fear of losing all the stability we have built. Yet if such a transition can be successfully made, then we see the fresh energy of the Eight, which implies not only enthusiasm about acquiring a new skill but also relief that we have not exhausted all our potentials, but can still continue to grow and make new things manifest.

On a divinatory level, the Eight of Pentacles augurs a period when the individual plays the role of the hard-working apprentice who is struggling to acquire a new skill. This card can suggest a talent which the individual has recently discovered and which is worthy of development and effort, or it can imply that a hobby could be developed into a profession. The individual may experience great enthusiasm and interest in some new field of work which requires him or her to become a hard-working trainee, often at a time of life when one 'ought' to be firmly established.

Nine of Pentacles

The card of the Nine of Pentacles portrays Daedalus standing with his hands folded in a posture of satisfaction, a self-congratulatory smile on his face. He has discarded his tunic and leather apron, and is now clothed in a rich ochre-coloured gown trimmed with gold. On his head rests a laurel wreath. On either side of him, richly laden vines climb up a wooden trellis, while in the distance can be seen green mountains and a calm blue sea. Beside the craftsman, piled on the ground, are nine golden pentacles.

The Nine of Pentacles portrays a state of great self-satisfaction. Daedalus has gambled on a dangerous venture, worked hard to develop it, taken the risks and suffered the attendant dangers, and now stands admiring the rewards which he has earned. What is important and different about the Nine of Pentacles is that the pleasure the craftsman feels in his wealth is not due to anyone else's applause or validation. This is the solitary enjoyment of good things, the pleasure in self-sufficiency and accomplishment which can only come from within oneself and which one offers to oneself. Daedalus can here justifiably say, 'I did it my way,' for his pile of wealth is really a symbol of the sense of self-worth which can only be acquired from within. Not only has the craftsman made peace with his shadowy past and his period of loss and exile; he has also outwitted King Minos, who became his enemy because of his decision to assist the queen and follow the will of the god Poseidon. The danger is now in the past; the craftsman can feel satisfaction that his efforts and his wits have ensured his survival and wealth and position for the rest of his life.

Thus the Nine of Pentacles is a card of reward and achievement in one's own eyes, and we know that even if no one else acknowledges the value of what has been achieved, it is worthy because we know it to be so from within. There is a permanence and indestructibility about the satisfaction embodied in the Nine which is not present in any other card in the Minor Arcana. This satisfaction is dependent upon nothing and no one outside oneself. Once built, it cannot be destroyed, even if the pile of wealth were to be taken away. The Nine of Pentacles is more than a card of worldly achievement. On a subtler level, it implies the finding of a deep and permanent sense of self-value, which has been earned through the hard work of meeting life's challenges on a material level and somehow surviving them all.

On a divinatory level, the Nine of Pentacles augurs a period where one may be justifiably pleased with oneself and with what one has been able to achieve. There is often a strong sense of solid identity, a feeling of one's unique abilities and the worth of one's life. This is not inflated, but based on a realistic appreciation of one's skills. This card reflects the solitary and self-sufficient enjoyment of good things, which does not depend upon anyone else's agreement or validation to provide pleasure and deep satisfaction.

Ten of Pentacles

The card of the Ten of Pentacles portrays Daedalus as an old man, his brown hair now liberally streaked with grey. He is comfortably seated with his children and grandchildren around him, the patriarch and founder of a line. On either side of him, mounted on vine-draped columns, hang ten golden pentacles, five to his left and five to his right. In his lap nestles an infant playing with a golden rattle. To his left stands a woman of around thirty, clothed in green and wearing a beautiful golden necklace. At his feet, a boy of ten plays with a toy golden horse. In the distance can be seen a landscape of rich green mountains and calm blue sea.

The Ten of Pentacles portrays a situation of permanence which outlasts the life of a single individual. Here the craftsman, secure in his position at the court of King Cocalus of Sicily, has at last put down roots and founded a dynasty. Not only has he accrued wealth and power, but he can pass his achievements on when it is his time to die, secure in the knowledge that his work will outlive him. The golden objects which he has made – the rattle, the necklace, the toy horse – are his gifts to the future, so that the process of manifestation which is embodied in all the cards of the Suit of Pentacles achieves its natural conclusion in an image of permanence which forms the individual's contribution to future generations. In some ways this is the deepest meaning of the process of manifesting creative ideas in form, for all individual life is transient and no man or woman lives forever; yet a sense of profound satisfaction and fulfilment may be achieved by the realization that one has built something enduring for the world which will come after. To the Suit of Wands, immortality lies in the imagination, and to the Suit of Swords it lies in the divine power of the mind; and to the Suit of Cups it lies in the experience of love, which touches on the transpersonal. But for the Suit of Pentacles only what is here is real, and it is this feeling that one has left a mark of some kind – that one's passing through life has not been a meaningless flicker that too soon vanishes – that often forms the kernel of what we call worldly ambition. Thus the apparent crass materialism and ambition which are often associated with earthly endeavours may have at their core a profound human need to offer something of oneself to life as a permanent marker of one's voyage through it. A life fully lived, as Daedalus' life has been, with both good and evil in it and a willingness to take on life's challenges fully regardless of the consequences rather than rotting peaceably in one's bed, can often lead to this experience of having fulfilled a destiny and left something which can be passed down to future generations.

On a divinatory level, the Ten of Pentacles suggests a period of ongoing contentment and security, and a sense of something permanent having been established which can be handed on to others. This may be a material inheritance of wealth or property, or it may be an artistic achievement such as a book or painting which one knows will live on and offer its value independent of one's own span of life.

The Court Cards

Page of Pentacles

The card of the Page of Pentacles portrays a boy of around twelve years of age, with dark brown hair and an olive complexion, dressed in a pale leaf-green tunic. He stands in a field where the new green growth of different varieties of vegetables, flowers and herbs is just showing above the ploughed furrows of rich dark soil. He holds a golden pentacle gently in both hands. Above him, the sky is a pale, delicate blue.

Here, in the card of the Page of Pentacles, we meet the element of earth in its most delicate and fragile beginnings – the nascent awareness of the senses, of nature, and of the capacity to manifest things in the world. This is embodied in the mythic figure of the boy Triptolemus, who was the son of King Celeus of Eleusis. One day the boy and his brothers were about their father's business in the fields, Triptolemus herding the king's cattle while his two brothers tended the sheep and the swine. These three saw a strange drama enacted. The earth suddenly gaped open, engulfing all of King Celeus' swine. Then a chariot drawn by black horses appeared, and dashed down the chasm. The chariot-driver's face was invisible, but his right arm was tightly clasped around a shrieking girl.

THE SUIT OF PENTACLES

What the three brothers had witnessed was the rape of Persephone by the dark god Hades, lord of the underworld, which story we have already encountered in the Major Arcana cards of the Empress and the High Priestess. Persephone's mother Demeter had travelled all over the world wearily seeking some news of her daughter's disappearance. When she arrived, disguised, at Eleusis, the boy Triptolemus alone recognized her, and gave her the information she needed, which had eluded her for so long. For this act of kindness the Earth Mother rewarded Triptolemus first by teaching him her worship and mysteries – in essence, the mysteries of nature and the death and regeneration of life through the seasonal cycles. She then supplied the boy with seed-corn, a wooden plough, and a serpent-drawn chariot, and sent him all over the world to teach mankind the art of agriculture.

Triptolemus, the Page of Pentacles, is an image of those early and delicate efforts to relate to the sensual world which must emerge first before any larger ambitions of a material kind can be pursued. In common with all the Pages of the Minor Arcana, the Page of Pentacles is a bud, a bare beginning, and like all buds this gentle, delicate beginning of recognition of the value of the material world must be nurtured and protected lest it be crushed through undervaluing and neglect. Often the Page of Pentacles can suggest the early interest in some new hobby, which starts as a mere idea or enthusiasm, but which if cared for and developed slowly and patiently may eventually become a full-blown vocation which yields both material and emotional rewards and fulfilment. We have all experienced these little enthusiasms – but how many of us really follow them up, and try the necessary first small steps which might lead to something greater? Triptolemus, the Page of Pentacles, is a serious child, responsible and hard-working as few children are; at a young age he is given care of his father's cattle, instead of playing like other boys. Thus the energy of the Page of Pentacles needs to be treated gently but seriously.

Likewise the image of Triptolemus may reflect the delicate beginnings of sensuality emerging, particularly if the individual has all his or her life undervalued this dimension of experience. The beginnings of sensual awareness in a more intellectual or imaginative temperament may be overlooked or despised, yet the myth of Triptolemus suggests that if the life of the body is recognized and valued as the boy recognizes and values the goddess Demeter, great rewards may emerge in the future. For many people this nascent awareness of the body may take the form of a desire to care for oneself better, through a better diet or exercise, or more time for relaxation, or an interest in gardening or caring for animals – playful things which lead to a deeper and stronger relationship with the earth itself.

When the Page of Pentacles appears in a spread, it marks the gathering together of energy which can eventually be used for building things in the world and for fulfilling the needs of the body. Sometimes money becomes available in small sums, which need to be saved and nurtured rather than thrown away as insignificant. Sometimes the individual takes up a new hobby which may later develop into a profession with time and careful work; or he or she may begin to care more for the body and take more interest in sensual pleasure and fulfilment. The message here, as with all the Pages, is that care, gentleness and time are needed to bring the potential to fruition.

Knight of Pentacles

The card of the Knight of Pentacles portrays a swarthy young man with dark brown hair, mounted on a stocky brown horse. He is dressed in a lime-green tunic and brown leather armour, and wears a brown leather helmet. In his right hand he holds a golden pentacle; in his left, a sheaf of wheat. Around him lie rolling pastures dotted with sheep, and an olive grove with beehives. Above him is a brilliant blue sky.

Here, in the card of the Knight of Pentacles, we meet the industrious, versatile, and changeable dimension of the element of earth, which is constantly in motion. This is embodied in the mythic figure of Aristaeus, who was called 'Guardian

THE SUIT OF PENTACLES

of the Flocks'. Aristaeus was the son of the sun-god Apollo, by a mortal woman called Kyrene, and when he was an infant he was given to the Earth Mother who fed him on nectar and ambrosia. The dryads or tree-nymphs taught Aristaeus how to curdle milk for cheese, build bee-hives, and make the oleaster yield the cultivated olive. These useful arts he taught to others while still a young man, travelling ceaselessly over North Africa and Greece, earning honours as he went.

When Aristaeus grew to maturity, the Muses in turn taught him the arts of healing and prophecy, and set him to watch over their sheep which grazed across the Plain of Phthia. It was here that he perfected the art of hunting. One day Aristaeus consulted the Delphic Oracle of his father Apollo, who told him to visit the island of Keos, where he would be greatly honoured. Setting sail at once, Aristaeus found that a plague had fallen upon the islanders because of secret murderers who were sheltering among them. Aristaeus put the murderers to death and the plague ceased, and the Keans showered him with gratitude. He then visited Arcadia, and later Tempe, but at Tempe all his bees began to die, and he was advised by his mother to find the old sea-god Proteus, who was a prophet, and force him to explain the reason for the catastrophe. Aristaeus duly found and captured Proteus, who told him that the bees' sickness was due to an unfortunate love-episode which resulted in the woman's accidental death, for which Aristaeus was being punished by the gods. In expiation he offered various sacrificial beasts to the offended deities, and from the rotting carcasses of the slaughtered animals a swarm of bees rose, which he captured and put into a hive. Aristaeus then continued his travels, to Libya and thence to Sardinia, and eventually to Sicily. Finally he went to Thrace, still restless and searching for further tasks to fulfil. Eventually he founded the city of Aristaeum, and died there honoured for his wisdom.

Aristaeus, the Knight of Pentacles, is an image of the human capacity for industry and diligent service. He is not really a hero, for he faces no dragons or dangerous quests, and his greatest challenge is the healing of his sick bees. But he is a powerful and creative figure nonetheless. The character of Aristaeus is that of the lover of the countryside, and friend of animals and all wild creatures, to whom no task is too menial provided it serves the life of nature. Although his aims are limited – Aristaeus could never be accused of the grandiose pride which afflicts so many Greek heroes and which is the cause of their glory and their ultimate downfall – yet he is kind and dependable, willing to work long and hard for the matters which concern him. Although virtually every figure in Greek myth is culpable of some rape, seduction, murder or some other crime, it is a peculiar trait of Aristaeus that he willingly accepts such a detailed and tiresome ritual and discharges it impeccably for the sake of a few bees.

Thus Aristaeus embodies that side of us which is humble enough to relate to the humblest forms of life, and which is always ready to learn more about the varied and complex faces of nature. The Knight of Pentacles is not a glamorous figure, but he is capable of great contentment because his achievements are always circumscribed by realism and humble aims. This is the quality which allows us to accept with good grace the job which may be boring yet which must be done, and to discharge faithfully the tasks of ordinary living. Aristaeus has no pretentions to divinity, yet he is a god's son and after his death is himself worshipped as divine.

When the Knight of Pentacles appears in a spread, it is time for the individual to develop that dimension of the personality which is comfortably and firmly anchored in the ordinary tasks of living. The Knight of Pentacles may enter one's life as an industrious, humble, gentle, hard-working young man, perhaps lacking in imagination but rich in the qualities of reliability and gentleness. But if such a person enters one's sphere, it may be seen as an opportunity to learn more about this side of oneself through the catalyst of another.

Queen of Pentacles

The card of the Queen of Pentacles portrays a beautiful woman with rich dark brown hair and brown eyes, wearing a sensuously draped russet robe and a golden crown. She

THE SUIT OF PENTACLES

is seated on a golden throne whose arms are engraved with the heads of bulls. In her right hand she holds a golden pentacle; in her left, a bunch of purple grapes. Around her lie ripe green and gold pastures, in which a herd of cattle can be seen grazing.

Here, in the card of the Queen of Pentacles, we meet the receptive, stable, sensuous dimension of the element of earth. This is embodied in the mythic figure of Queen Omphale, whose name means 'navel'. Omphale appears in the cycle of stories concerning the hero Heracles, who at a low point in his career was taken to Asia and offered for sale as a nameless slave – a far cry from the hero as we first met him in the Major Arcana card of Strength. He was bought by Omphale, queen of Lydia, a woman with a good eye for a bargain; and he served her faithfully for three years, ridding Asia Minor of the bandits who infested the countryside.

Omphale had been bequeathed her kingdom by her late husband, and ruled it ably because of her pragmatic and powerful character. She bought Heracles as a lover rather than a fighter, and he fathered three sons on her. She made the best of her time with the hero by indulging herself thoroughly. Reports reached Greece that Heracles had discarded his lion pelt and instead wore jewelled necklaces, golden bracelets, a woman's turban, purple shawl and a Maeonian girdle. There he sat – the story went – teasing wool from a wool-basket or spinning the thread, trembling when his mistress scolded him. He let himself be combed and manicured by Omphale's maids, while she dressed up in his lion pelt and wielded his club and bow.

One day the pair visited some vineyards, and the god Pan, whom we have met already in the Major Arcana card of the Devil, caught sight of them from a high hill. Falling in love with Omphale, the goat-footed god bade farewell to his nymphs and declared undying love for the Lydian queen. Omphale, well aware that Pan pursued her, suggested to Heracles as they retired for the night in a grotto that they exchange clothes. At midnight Pan crept into the grotto, found someone whom he thought was Omphale lying asleep, and with trembling hands tried to assault what turned out to be a furious Heracles. The hero kicked Pan across the grotto, and he and Omphale laughed until they cried to see the goat-god sprawled in a corner nursing his bruises. Since that day Pan has abhorred clothes, and summons his officials naked to his rites.

Omphale, the Queen of Pentacles, is an image of feminine strength and sensuality, which can enslave even an untamed brute like Heracles. In one sense she represents the sensuality of the body itself – hence her name, for the Greeks believed that passion was centred in the navel – and which is present in both men and women. This is not simply craving for physical satisfaction, but a primordial force which possesses both dignity and power. In serving Queen Omphale, Heracles passes through a kind of initiation – and we too, when we encounter the Queen of Pentacles within ourselves, must bow to the power of the instincts and acknowledge that even the highest mind and most rarefied spirituality exist in a body which is made of earth. Omphale is not, however, merely a sensualist. She is a ruler in her own right, prepared to be generous but always pragmatic and protective of her own wealth and territory. Her purchase of the hero as a lover is made not because no other lovers are available, but because she wants the best. Thus she may also be taken as an image of self-value, because Omphale treats herself and her body as well as her country with care and lavish generosity. She possesses the endurance and stability of the earth itself, and although sensuality alone cannot fill a life, Omphale is an image of great importance and value.

When the Queen of Pentacles appears in a spread, it is time for the individual to learn about the full expression of his or her sensuality, the value of the body, and the importance of those pleasures which preserve and enrich life. The individual may also be called upon to learn to sustain and preserve material resources, holding conditions stable and secure and husbanding money and energy. The Queen of Pentacles may enter one's life as a strong, sensual woman, self-sufficient and hard-working yet generous and willing to indulge herself and others if it suits her purposes. But if such a woman enters one's life, it suggests that these qualities are trying to emerge from within oneself.

King of Pentacles

The card of the King of Pentacles portrays a swarthy man with dark brown hair and beard, solidly built, and obviously contented with his powerful worldly position. He is seated on a golden throne whose arms are engraved with the heads of goats. Behind him rises a fortified castle, built of stone and draped with vines. In front of the castle his menials and attendants stand ready to serve him. In his hands he holds one golden pentacle, while beneath his feet lies a heap of golden coins – tiny pentacles, his accumulation of worldly wealth. He is richly but tastefully robed in gold brocade, and wears a golden crown. On the grass beside him, a brown goat grazes.

Here, in the card of the King of Pentacles, we meet the active, dynamic dimension of the element of earth. This is embodied by the mythic King Midas, a pleasure-loving king of Macedonia. In his infancy, a procession of ants was observed carrying grains of wheat up the side of his cradle and placing them between his lips as he slept – a prodigy which the soothsayers read as an omen of the great wealth that would accrue to him.

Midas ruled as a wise and pious king, and his kindness to the drunken satyr Silenos, tutor of the god Dionysos, earned him the gratitude of the unpredictable god. Dionysos offered to grant Midas one wish, to which Midas replied without hesitation: 'Pray grant that all I touch be turned into gold.' The king soon regretted this indiscretion, for not only stones, flowers, and the furnishings of his house turned to gold, but when he sat down to table, so did the food he ate and the water he drank. Midas soon begged to be released from his wish, because he was rapidly dying of hunger and thirst. Dionysos, highly entertained but compassionate, told him to visit the source of the River Pactolus, where Midas washed himself and was at once freed from the golden touch, but the sands of the River Pactolus are bright with gold to this day.

Midas, the King of Pentacles, is an image of human ambition. He is our aspiration to status and worldly achievement, our desire for power and recognition in the eyes of others, our need for material security and

THE SUIT OF PENTACLES

our pride in having worked to earn what we have. This ambition is also a dynamic spirit, for it is not content with comfort, but must have challenges. In the myth, Midas earns the reward of the god Dionysos through an act of kindness, sympathy for the drunken old satyr whom everyone else despises and ridicules. This hints at an important truth about worldly success: It depends not only upon hard work and cleverness, but also upon recognizing and understanding those aspects of human behaviour which are lazy, indolent, drunken and bestial. Only by tolerating and containing these things, portrayed by the old satyr, can the foundations of worldly power and authority be secure, for otherwise the individual can be corrupted simply because he is unconscious of his own potential for corruption. The King of Pentacles has reached the top because he has the right qualities of leadership, authority, realism and discipline to overcome the obstacles in his path. But as the myth suggests, he must also learn a hard lesson about his own greed. Midas already has enough and more; he is a rich and powerful king, and does not exactly go about in threadbare clothes. He is entitled to be ambitious, but his ambition cannot be put before everything, or he will die of hunger and thirst. Having learned his lesson, the king is content to bask in his rewards. He is an unashamed materialist, and when we encounter this figure in ourselves we encounter our own materialism, even if previously we had believed ourselves to be idealists with contempt for such crassness. This king is healthy and strong. Although, as with every card in the Tarot, one cannot remain stuck in a single facet of life, the encounter with material ambition and its challenges and rewards can be a productive and healing one – even if it means one must, in some form, experience Midas' hard lesson.

When the King of Pentacles appears in a spread, it is time for the individual to take up the challenge of worldly things. But inner movements often need a catalyst, and therefore the King of Pentacles may enter one's life as an earthy, strong, successful individual – one who has the 'Midas touch', who has the gift of manifesting creative ideas in the world. But such an individual is a catalyst for one's own developing material self-confidence.

READING THE CARDS

What the Tarot Can and Cannot Do

The Tarot cards cannot predict a fixed and fated future. They are a series of images which describe the qualities of the moment when an individual consults them with a particular problem or situation in mind. The Greeks, naturally, had a word for it – *kairos*, which means 'the right moment', and which describes the idea that every moment in time possesses peculiar and unique characteristics and qualities. We must dispense with our typical twentieth-century Western view of time in order to understand what the Tarot cards really do, and look instead toward ancient philosophy and the beliefs of the East, where time is seen not in terms of quantity (a moment is a measurement, one-sixtieth of an hour) but in terms of quality (a moment is a living thing, possessing its own identity and meaning). Seen through the lens of this world-view, life possesses an underlying and secret connectedness or relatedness, and all levels of life, animate and inanimate, conscious and unconscious, inner and outer, are really part of a living whole. Therefore life will reflect, on all the levels of its existence, the same qualities in a given moment of time. Thus the ancient methods of divination, such as astrology, the Tarot and the *I Ching*, do not seek to 'predict' an already written future, but concern themselves instead with how the true inner quality and meaning of the moment might be reflected and therefore deciphered through symbolic forms such as planets, coins or cards.

This is a difficult concept for the Western mind to grasp, but if we attempt it, it will help us to clarify an issue about which there is much misunderstanding among students of the Tarot. Not only does a moment have particular qualities, but it has a past and a future which belong under the general umbrella of those qualities. There are situations and choices in the past which have led up to that moment, and of which that moment is the consequence; and there are situations and choices in the future which spring directly from our response to

READING THE CARDS

that moment, and are in turn affected by our present choices. Therefore it makes sense to understand all we can about how we landed ourselves in a particular situation, for this understanding will in turn affect how we respond to life, and therefore what the next 'moment' will bring. Over the situations and choices which pertain to a given moment hangs a particular archetypal meaning, for there is nothing we do or experience that has not been done or experienced before; and it is this archetypal meaning which the Tarot cards can reveal.

The past, present and future which are implied in a particular Tarot card reading tend to express a period of around six months. Thus, the 'moment' which we have been considering is a period of time, including the past – the choices, motives and experiences which have led to it – the present when the cards are consulted, and the future – which is the natural outgrowth of the forces at work in the present. The cards do not describe concrete events in a 'fated' way, but instead illustrate influences and opportunities and hidden motives – some of which may or may not crystallize in external events or persons – which the individual may then try to understand and work with in as creative a way as possible. Because it is the quality of the moment which is described, the individual can, by seeking to penetrate to the deeper meaning of the moment, cast a more conscious influence on the future of that moment, thus affecting with increased awareness the future which is unfolding. In this sense we create our own fates, or rather, what we are fates our futures. Fate to the Greeks was not a random and capricious selection of events which happened to a person, but rather a complex and infinite web of choices, responses and consequences extending throughout time, back into the past and forward into the future, most of which remained unconscious unless the individual sought to bring deeper awareness to his or her inner life.

Because the 'fate' which the Tarot cards describe is largely rooted in the unconscious, we do not ordinarily have access to it. But the images of the Tarot cards can help us to make a connection with it, and therefore the cards reflect back to us the *a priori* knowledge of the unconscious, which holds the secret key to the meaning of the moment and therefore knows the probable future outcome of that moment. By reading the Tarot cards, one can receive help in reading the complex patterns and movements of the unconscious, and this new relationship between conscious ego and the hidden inner world allows us to bring to the moment – and therefore to our situation in the moment – a deeper insight and greater possibilities of response and choice.

Making a Relationship With the Cards

Because the images of the Tarot cards are so ancient and so deeply connected with the innermost patterns of human development, the cards merit respect. They are not toys, but in a sense are sacred images, not because they are 'supernatural', but because, like a piece of great art or literature, they reflect our most profound conflicts, needs and aspirations. The individual who wishes to learn to work with and tap the creative potentials of the cards therefore needs to cultivate an attitude of respect toward the archetypal dimension of life which they represent, and this translates in ordinary life as a respect for the symbolic world, of which the cards themselves are a representative. The intelligent reader thus tries to establish a kind of 'relationship' with the cards, where they hold a special place and are not simply amusing pieces of paper which are allowed to grow dirty, ragged and neglected.

For this reason, many professional readers keep their Tarot cards wrapped in a special cloth, in a special place when not in use. With THE MYTHIC TAROT is included such a cloth, marked with a pattern of one of the traditional spreads of the cards, which we will explain in greater detail later. This cloth is our way of helping the student to begin to develop a respectful relationship with the cards. Traditionally, the Tarot cards were kept wrapped in black silk, the rationale behind this being that black is a neutral colour, keeping outside 'vibrations' – both negative and positive – away from the cards. Whether or not this is true,

READING THE CARDS

the importance of some kind of ritual in the use of the cards needs to be acknowledged, for on a psychological level ritual attunes our minds and allows the intuition to come into play. Like a religious ritual, the ritual of keeping the cards in their own special place and of wrapping and unwrapping them in their own special cloth can become an important focus of concentration – whether or not one believes in 'vibrations'. It is a symbol of the unique and valued place which the cards hold, and the importance of their images.

Laying out a Spread

The process of selecting a small number of cards from the entire Tarot deck of seventy-eight, and setting them out in a pattern to be interpreted, is called laying out a spread. The idea behind this is that the deck, as we have seen, contains a pictorial description of the entirety of life's complex journey, and by selecting a minimal number of cards – usually ten – the seeker is, symbolically, reflecting his or her own passage through a particular part of that overall journey in the present moment. In other words, the immediate situation, its origins and its probable outcome will be reflected in this small portion of the entire deck.

There are many different kinds of spreads, and different people have evolved their favourite patterns over many centuries. The student is referred to the book list in the Bibliography for a more complete description of the many Tarot spreads in use. The particular spread which we will illustrate here is one of the oldest and most popular, and is known as the Celtic Cross. This spread contains selections from both the Major and Minor Arcana, for the individual chooses from the entire deck; therefore the selection reflects life on both the deeper archetypal level and the more ordinary everyday level. As we have stated before, we do not use the technique of reversed cards, because each card contains within it a dark and a light dimension; and this can be determined by the card's position in the overall spread.

READING THE CARDS

The black cloth which is enclosed in the package of THE MYTHIC TAROT illustrates the placement of the ten selected cards in a pattern, numbered according to the order in which they should be chosen. To learn to lay out the cards in the Celtic Cross spread, the reader will need first to spread out the black cloth so that the pattern can be easily read.

The seeker – the person who wishes to consult the cards – should have a question in mind, even if this question is vague and difficult to formulate. The reader does not necessarily have to know this question, but the seeker should know it, because on some unconscious level the cards which are chosen will reflect that question.

The reader shuffles the cards thoroughly, and then spreads the seventy-eight cards out in a fan-shape, face down, on the table.

The seeker is invited to choose ten cards from the seventy-eight. Because they lie face down, the seeker cannot consciously know which cards he or she has selected.

The reader then takes the ten cards, in the order selected still face down, and places them in their correct positions as marked on the black cloth. The first card chosen should be placed in Position One, and so on.

The reader may now turn over the cards, beginning with Position One, until the images of all ten cards are visible.

Reading the Spread

The ten positions of the cards in the Celtic Cross spread have been given traditional names which help us to understand their meaning. Each placement describes a particular area of life where a certain influence and inner and outer situation are occurring. We will now explain the ten positions and what they mean.

POSITION ONE is sometimes called the Covering Card and sometimes called the Significator. We will use the term Significator because the card which has been chosen for this position will reflect the situation, inner

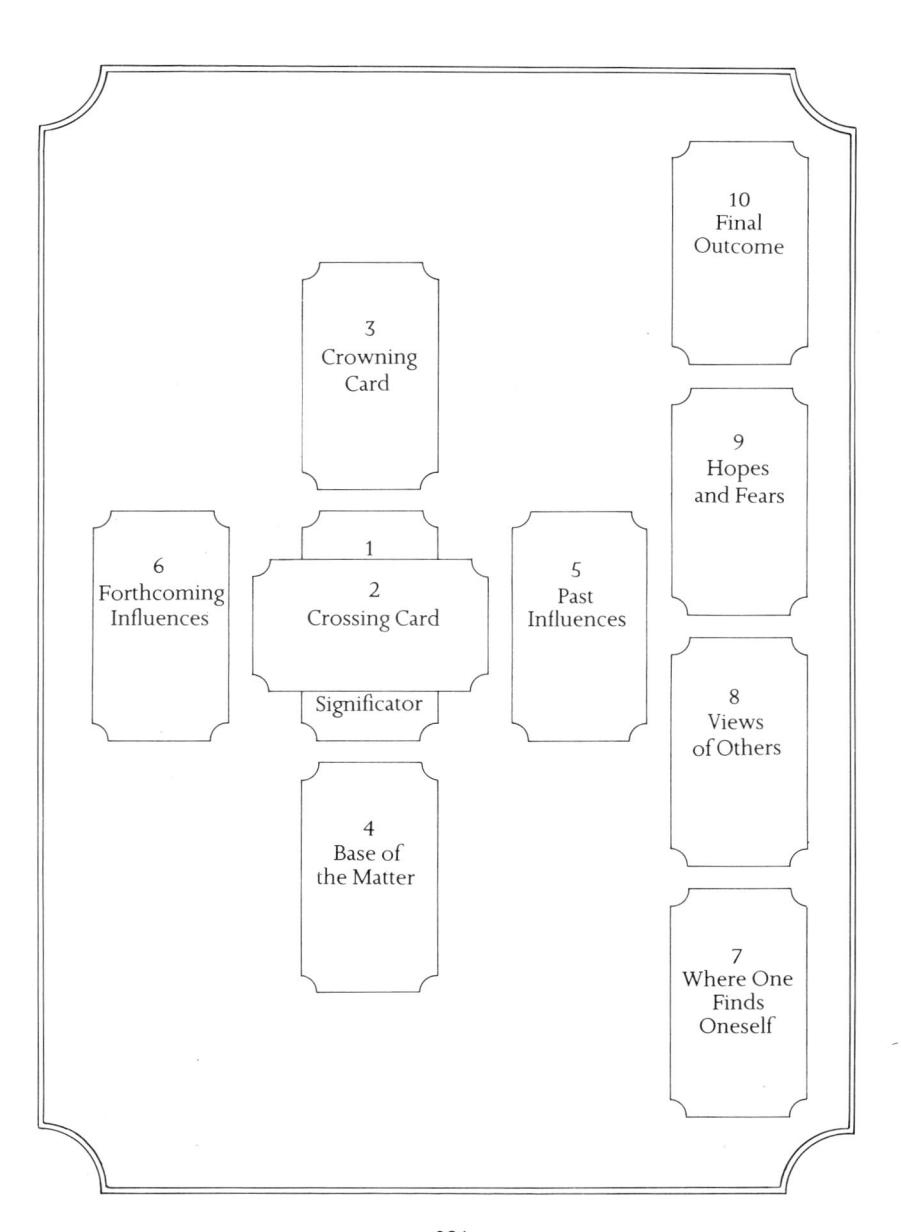

	3 Crowning Card		10 Final Outcome
			9 Hopes and Fears
6 Forthcoming Influences	1 2 Crossing Card Significator	5 Past Influences	8 Views of Others
	4 Base of the Matter		7 Where One Finds Oneself

and outer, in which the individual finds himself or herself at the present moment.

POSITION TWO is called the Crossing Card, and describes that situation, inner and outer, which is generating conflict and obstruction in the immediate present. It is the thing which 'crosses' the seeker, and indicates the apparent nature of the problem. However, the Crossing Card is not necessarily negative in meaning, but simply represents the situation which is generating the conflict and stirring up matters. In a sense, it prevents the Significator from fully expressing, and causes blockage in life.

POSITION THREE is called the Crowning Card. It is apparent simply from its visual appearance – hanging directly over the Significator – that the card which appears in this position describes the atmosphere and situation which hang over the seeker in the immediate present. What is at the crown of something is what appears in full view on top; and thus the card which appears here reflects what is out on the surface and immediately apparent in the seeker's life.

POSITION FOUR is called the Base of the Matter. This describes the inner and outer situation, drive, instinct or aspiration which is really behind the apparent surface situation reflected by the Crowning Card. What is at the base is really what is at the root of the psyche, and often this card comes as a surprise to the seeker, who may not have been aware of an unconscious motivation which needs to be brought into awareness. We do not always act or feel things for the reasons we think, and the card which appears at the Base of the Matter will often contradict the apparent reason for our dilemma at the time of consulting the cards.

POSITION FIVE is called Past Influences. The card which appears in this position describes the inner and outer situation which is now passing out of the seeker's life. In the past it had been important, perhaps representing a set of values which the individual held in high esteem; but now it has lost its potency, and the seeker needs to be able to let go

READING THE CARDS

of whatever this card represents before the new future developments can be integrated creatively into life.

POSITION SIX is called Forthcoming Influences. The card which appears in this position describes the inner and outer situation which is about to manifest in the seeker's life. This is not a long-term prognosis of a future outcome, but rather a description of the currents at work in the immediate future.

POSITION SEVEN is called Where One Finds Oneself, and it is a kind of future extension of Position One, the Significator. The card which appears in this position describes the attitude or inner state of affairs in which the seeker will soon find himself or herself. This card, like the Significator, describes a set of attitudes or inner qualities, and will often represent what needs to be developed as well as what is likely to unfold.

POSITION EIGHT is called the Views of Others, and it describes the image which those around us – friends and family – hold of our situation and ourselves. The card which appears in this position will usually imply what kind of response to our situation we can expect from others, and also what we ourselves have been unconsciously doing to project such an image to the world outside. Often an individual who is going through problems of one kind or another does not receive the understanding and sympathy from friends and loved ones that he or she hopes for, and the card in Position Eight can often tell us why not; for this is the view the world has of us, and it may contradict the way we feel as easily as it may honestly reflect our situation.

POSITION NINE is called Hopes and Fears. Both hopes and fears can be described by one card, for all the cards in the Tarot deck have a double face.

POSITION TEN is called the Final Outcome. The word 'final' can be misleading here, for nothing is absolutely final, as we have seen in the circular journey of the Fool; and the card which appears in this position describes a situation not of lifelong permanence, but one which is the natural outgrowth of whatever we are going through at the moment. As we have said, this 'final outcome' may cover a period of around six months.

We can now turn to two example spreads to explore in further detail how to read the cards.

Two Example Spreads

The first example which we will use to illustrate the reading of the cards is that of a twenty-eight-year-old woman, who wished to consult the cards regarding problems concerning her marriage and her work. She and her husband had been married for several years but as yet had no children; they lived in a London flat and both had full-time jobs. This woman, whom we will call Celia, was the fashion editor for a popular women's magazine, while her husband worked as an accountant. Both were dissatisfied with their life in a city flat and had been discussing the possibility of moving to the country, partly because of the boredom of their jobs, and partly because the marriage seemed to have reached a state of stagnation. Obviously some kind of change was needed; but Celia was confused about what to do, for although her husband spoke of starting a landscaping business in the country, she herself had no clear idea of what work might suit her that could be done away from the busy metropolis to which she was accustomed, and which might fulful her creative potential.

This background gives us a picture of someone at the proverbial crossroads, unclear as to the direction of the future and full of anxiety about the state of her personal life; yet willing to make a commitment to the future if only she could find some sense of which way to go.

Celia chose ten cards which comprised the following spread:

JUSTICE appearing as the Significator suggests that she needs – and is

TEMPERANCE
EIGHT OF CUPS
THE WORLD
KING OF CUPS
JUSTICE
NINE OF WANDS
TEN OF PENTACLES
THE EMPEROR
THE SUN
PAGE OF SWORDS

READING THE CARDS

beginning – to sit down and think clearly, coldly and rationally about her problem. As this is a Major Arcana card, portrayed by the steely image of the godess Athene, the implication is that developing this capacity for detached reflection is important not only for the immediate situation, but as a quality which has perhaps not been too developed in Celia in the past and which has now appeared as something very necessary for her to integrate into her character for the future. Consulting the cards is in a way the beginning of that detached reflection.

NINE OF WANDS appearing as the Crossing Card suggests that Celia has had to face a continual run of conflicts and obstructions to her hopes and desires for the future, and now she is exhausted and uncertain of whether she has the strength to go through any more crises to reach her vision of a better life. Yet this card also implies that, if only she will try, she will find that the necessary reserves of strength will be available to weather the storm. This card portrays Jason's ship, the Argo, making the final difficult passage between the Clashing Rocks before it arrives safely home; and the implication here is that Celia has one last struggle to pass through before she finds what she is looking for.

EIGHT OF CUPS appearing as the Crowning Card suggests that a sense of emotional disappointment is making it difficult for Celia to look clearly at her possibilities. The Eight of Cups portrays Psyche abandoning hope of reconciliation with Eros, and descending in despair into the underworld; and the implication here is that Celia might have brought many fantasies and expectations into her marriage which have proven to be unworkable, and she is still suffering from a sense of disillusionment and hopelessness about the future of the relationship.

The SUN appearing as the Base of the Matter symbolizes Celia's burning desire for individual creative expression as well as meaning in her life. This is at present frustrated, which may be the reason why she is so dissatisfied and also perhaps why she has expected so much from her husband and marriage in the past. The Sun expresses something

READING THE CARDS

important, hopeful and optimistic about Celia's character beyond the present crisis; that she needs to shine in her own right, and to be recognized as a creative individual.

TEN OF PENTACLES appearing in the position of Past Influences suggests that Celia's attachment to material security must now be allowed to loosen if she is to find real fulfilment in the future. This card portrays the craftsman Daedalus, wealthy and successful, at the head of a happy dynasty to whom he can pass down his wealth. The financial contentment and 'respectability' which this image portrays have been very important to Celia in the past, but she might need to learn to place less value on such things if she is to satisfy her need for individual creative expression.

KING OF CUPS appearing in the position of Forthcoming Influences suggests that soon a new direction will open up, either through an individual (perhaps a teacher or someone interested in spheres such as counselling), or through therapy. Celia's own masculine spirit seems to be inclining towards a much more introverted and internal world of interest. The presence of a Court Card in this place suggests that an actual person may very well be the catalyst for these new interests developing; but if such a person does enter Celia's life, it is because she herself is moving toward an entirely new sphere of interest.

PAGE OF SWORDS appearing in the place of Where One Finds Oneself suggests that Celia may find herself in a troubled and irritable frame of mind. The Pages of the Minor Arcana all imply the beginnings of some new quality or direction, and here, reflected by the Suit of Swords, it is the quality of the developing intellect; and Celia is beginning to question views which she has previously held blindly, and is becoming intellectually restless and in need of some new line of study or development. Thus initially she may be quarrelsome and subject to gossip by others – those friends and loved ones who cannot understand why she is changing and resent her progress where they themselves might be stuck. She may be defensive and prone to pick quarrels because she has not yet developed the insight and confidence to wholeheartedly pursue the new values that are emerging.

THE EMPEROR appearing in the View of Others suggests that, to others, Celia seems to be successful, powerful and 'on top', and her dissatisfaction might therefore not meet with a great deal of sympathy in her immediate circle. From the outside, she seems to have everything – a good marriage, a beautiful home, a successful job, position, prestige and power. That she herself is frustrated and unfulfilled does not meet the eye of the world, which sees a Major Arcana card which is concerned with power and position in society. Celia herself has perhaps tried unconsciously to project this image, and because Zeus, the Emperor, is an image of the archetypal father, it is perhaps to please her father that she has created this 'persona' for others.

THE WORLD appearing in the place of Hopes and Fears suggests that Celia is being driven by an archetypal urge for completeness, and wants to become a whole person. It is not just material rewards she is after, but the sense of being complete – someone who uses all of herself in response to life. Her ambitions and expectations are therefore very high, and spring from a profound root, although not necessarily identifiable in worldly terms. The fear of becoming whole at the same time may reflect the anxiety that such a state will allow no room for her marriage; for a woman who can express both masculine and feminine sides often threatens the men in her life. Thus, Celia wants nothing less than everything – but fears it at the same time.

TEMPERANCE appearing in the place of Final Outcome suggests that the direction in which Celia is moving augurs well for the possibility of a balanced relationship in which there is some compromise and some genuine feeling exchange. This Major Arcana card, portraying Iris, the goddess of the rainbow, implies that an important change is trying to occur within Celia's psyche, whereby her capacity to function in relationship will develop into a more compassionate and human expression, free of many of the rigid expectations which are characteris-

READING THE CARDS

tic of the past and the source of many of her problems with her husband. Thus a hopeful and promising card sums up the direction in which life is moving for Celia.

The second example which we will use to illustrate the reading of the cards is that of a forty-five-year-old man, a medical doctor by profession, who had recently left his marriage and children and emigrated to England from Australia. This man, whom we will call Alan, wished to pursue an interest in alternative healing, with the idea of training in acupuncture or homeopathy and establishing a practise in London utilizing both his orthodox and unorthodox medical approaches. He was confused and still in considerable conflict about the separation from his family, although he felt on a deep level that he had made the right decision; but he was subject to bad depressions and feelings of grief and loneliness, although the parting was amicable and recently another woman had entered his life. He wished to know whether he was on the right track professionally, and also whether he would be able to move out of the disturbed emotional state and give his new relationship a chance.

Alan chose ten cards which comprised the following spread:

ACE OF PENTACLES suggests that Alan has a great deal of energy available in both the inner and outer worlds for a fresh effort at building something solid in his life. This card, because it implies resources and possibly money made available to the individual for a new project, augurs well for Alan's desire to branch into alternative medicine, for it seems likely that he will find material and personal support. The Ace of Pentacles, portrayed by the powerful earth-god Poseidon, is a hopeful and affirmative augury of the new direction Alan has chosen to take in his life.

SEVEN OF WANDS suggests that the problem spot for Alan is the conflict

READING THE CARDS

that will inevitably ensue with opponents within his profession. This is the card of 'stiff competition', portrayed by Jason battling with King Aeetes for possession of the Golden Fleece. This implies that Alan will have to be prepared to meet with conflict with his fellows, either because others want the place he wants, or because he might antagonize those of his profession who are more conservative and closed to new methods of healing. This conflict may also reflect an inner battle within Alan – between his intuitive new vision, symbolized by the fiery hero Jason, and the conservative 'old order', symbolized by King Aeetes, who had the Fleece first. Therefore Alan will need to be prepared for opposition from within himself as well as from outside, for this is the problem which 'crosses' his powerful urge to begin a new life.

DEATH appearing as the Crowning Card reflects the state of depression and unhappiness which Alan is now in. This is a Major Arcana card, which suggests that Alan is experiencing an archetypal dimension of life – the mourning which comes whenever a chapter of life is closed and one must leave behind the past to go naked and uncertain into the future. The presence of this card also implies that Alan might not have given sufficient time for mourning his loss. Separation from a family is no easy matter and although Alan feels he has made the right choice, the past must be mourned for.

QUEEN OF PENTACLES implies the presence in Alan's life of a woman, who in some way might be a catalyst for the new direction he wishes to take. His new relationship involved a strong and financially independent woman, herself divorced, who was very willing to offer him the emotional support and encouragement which he needed at this vulnerable stage of his life. She might also represent the development of a greater sensuality within Alan himself.

FOUR OF SWORDS suggests that Alan has just passed through a period of withdrawal and reflection, and has been gathering his strength to meet the challenges that lie ahead of him. But this period is now passing, and soon he will be able to move outward into life.

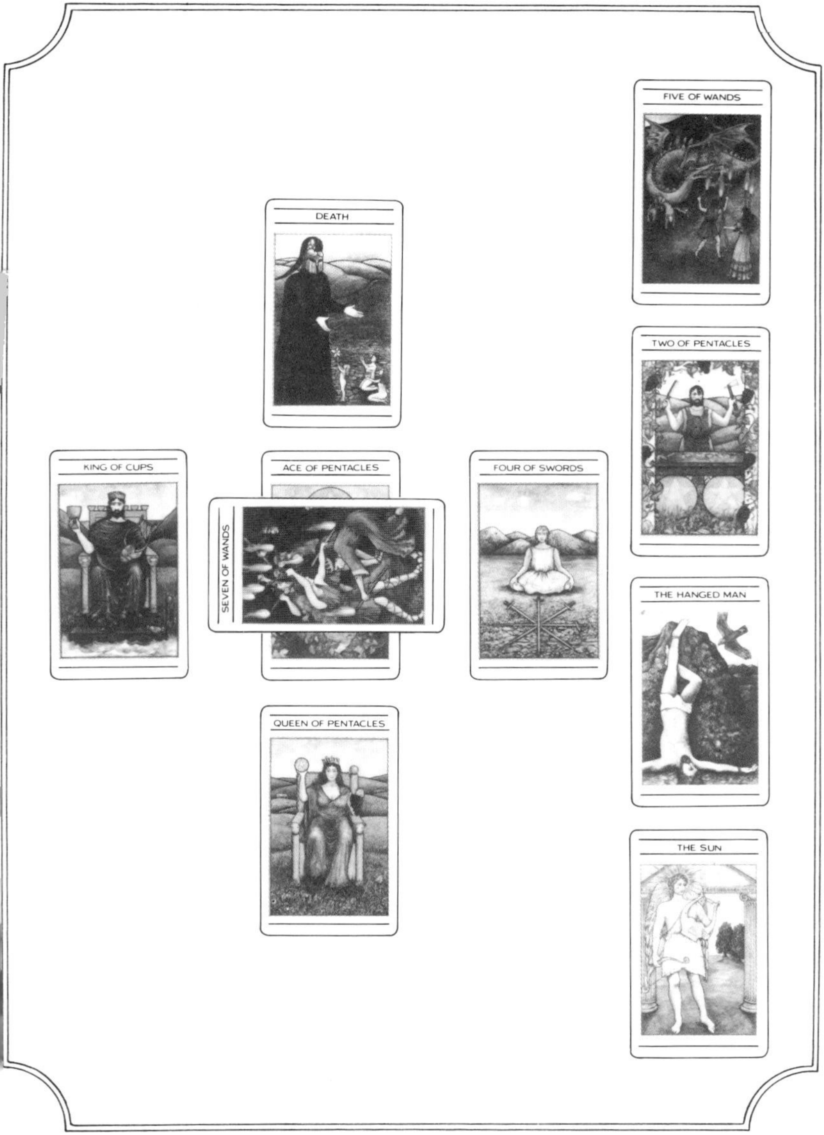

FIVE OF WANDS
DEATH
TWO OF PENTACLES
KING OF CUPS
ACE OF PENTACLES
SEVEN OF WANDS
FOUR OF SWORDS
THE HANGED MAN
QUEEN OF PENTACLES
THE SUN

READING THE CARDS

KING OF CUPS suggests the same thing that it did in Celia's spread – that Alan is being drawn toward the inner world of the feelings and the psyche, and that his interest in alternative healing might very well include some investigation of depth psychology in addition to the healing methods he intends to pursue. A man may enter Alan's life as a catalyst for this developing line of interest – perhaps a friend who is involved in such things, or a teacher or therapist. But this is also an image of what Alan himself is becoming – for he is drawing nearer to the inner realm, having left behind him not only his personal past but also his attachment to the healing of the body without the soul.

THE SUN suggests that Alan will probably experience a burst of great hope and optimism, because he is beginning to connect with an archetypal principle of meaning. This Major Arcana card is portrayed by Apollo, who among his other attributes was the god of healing; and this implies that in choosing to explore more deeply the meaning of healing, Alan will make a relationship with the profound resilience and creativity of the human spirit which will prove essential not only for his future work but for his own healing as well.

THE HANGED MAN suggests that, in the world's eyes, Alan has made a great sacrifice in exchange for an unknown and uncertain future. This Major Arcana card, portrayed by Prometheus, who stole fire from the gods to give to mankind, represents the giving up of something of value in the hope that something better, more meaningful and more worthwhile might come to take its place; but the future is full of uncertainty, and it is the uncertainty which those around Alan perceive. This is very much in accord with how Alan experiences himself, although the placement of THE SUN suggests that he also has a profound conviction of the meaning of his path – which those around him might not immediately see or understand.

TWO OF PENTACLES suggests that Alan is aiming toward the development of new skills. He may pass through a period of financial instability, where he is required to juggle time, energy and resources to make things work; and he seems to have some anxiety about this, reflected by the instability of the card in the place of Fears as well as Hopes. But this Minor Arcana card is not a card of loss. It portrays Daedalus in his workshop, at the beginning of his climb, developing his skills and inventing new tools. If Alan is willing to submit to a period of movement and change in his status and material security, then he will probably find that he does not suffer unduly, but will emerge with a new set of skills to help him in the future.

FIVE OF WANDS in the place of Final Outcome is an inconclusive card, reflecting the great dragon-fight of Jason in order to obtain the Golden Fleece. Here the meaning seems to be that Alan may find himself at odds with the collective, which, in the sense that his collective is the medical profession, will very likely make things difficult for him – as it tends to do with alternative healing in general. He will have a hard struggle on his hands, and the question he must ask himself is: Am I up to the struggle? If the answer to this question is Yes, then we would encourage Alan to continue to pursue his chosen interest, in full awareness that his path in the outer world may not be easy for some time.

READING THE CARDS

Conclusion

We have shown in this chapter how the Tarot cards reflect not only the direction of an individual's life at the time he or she consults the cards, but also those deeper unconscious motivations from the past which have helped to create the present situation. Although we are all individuals with a unique personality and a unique destiny, the experiences that life offers us are not infinitely varied in essence, but only in form; for they follow certain patterns which are ancient and inbuilt in all of us, and which are part of the process of living as human beings. These patterns have been expressed from time immemorial in the language of symbols – in the rich and beautiful tapestry of myths from many nations and cultures, in the religious images which inspire us, and in the equally rich and inspiring designs of the great symbolic systems such as the Tarot. Far from making us feel as though we are only repeating others, a knowledge and appreciation of the Fool's journey offers a sense of dignity and meaning to life's most difficult challenges, for we learn that there is beauty, order and purpose in even the darkest, most sordid and most banal events in our lives. Mythic images place us in relationship with the boundless inner world of the unconscious, which is modern psychology's way of describing what once – in less rational and scientific times – was understood as relationship with the divine.

Thus the imagery and meaning of the Tarot, which are best expressed through the ancient myths that gave birth to it, are neither 'supernatural' nor 'occult', but deeply and profoundly human and natural, and available to us all if we only take the time to look and learn.

We can find no better way to close our description of the Fool's journey than with these lines from the great poet T. S. Eliot:

> *And the end of all our exploring*
> *Will be to arrive where we started*
> *And know the place for the first time.*

FURTHER READING

Douglas, Alfred. *The Tarot*, Penguin Books Ltd., Harmondsworth, 1972
Pollack, Rachel. *Seventy Eight Degrees of Wisdom*, The Aquarian Press Ltd., Wellingborough, Northants, 1980
Waite, A. E *The Pictorial Key to the Tarot*, Rider, London, 1971
Hudson, Paul. *The Devil's Picturebook*. Sphere Books, London, 1972
Yates, Frances. *The Art of Memory*, Peregrine Books, Harmondsworth, 1969
New Larousse Encyclopedia of Mythology, Hamlyn Publishing Group, London, 1959
Frazer, Sir James. *The Golden Bough*, Macmillan, London, 1922.
Graves, Robert. *The Greek Myths*, Penguin Books Ltd., Harmondsworth, 1972
Graves, Robert. *The White Goddess*, Vintage Books, New York, 1961
Jung, C. G. *The Archetypes and the Collective Unconscious*, Vol. 9. Part 1, Routledge & Kegan Paul, London, 1959
Jung, C. G. *Psychological Types*, Vol. 6, Routledge & Kegan Paul, London, 1971

ACKNOWLEDGEMENTS

The authors acknowledge with thanks the help and encouragement received from Barbara Levy during their work on this project.
Eddison/Sadd Editions acknowledge contributions from the following people:

Editorial Director   Ian Jackson
Creative Director   Nick Eddison
Copy Editor and Proofreader   Jocelyn Selson
Designer   Amanda Barlow